Gjirokastra

the essential guide

servation
ment
tion

Contents

Acknowledgements
The Gjirokastra Conservation and Development Organization (GCDO) is very grateful to the Packard Humanities Institute whose generous and continued support has made this publication possible. The GCDO wishes to thank the Gjirokastra Municipality, especially the Mayor Flamur Bime, the Albanian Institute of Monuments, Spartak Drasa (Director of the Regional Directorate of National Culture), Raimond Kola (Director of the Gjirokastra Administration and Coordination Office), Engjëll Serjani (Director of the Antigoneia National Park), and Nevila Nika (Director of the General Directorate of Archives of Albania), for their support. In addition, the GCDO would like to thank Ilir Gjipali, Roberto Perna and Konstantinos Zachos for their help and advice. Richard Hodges, Diana Ndrenika and Louise Schofield are also owed a debt of gratitude. Thanks are also due to Andy Crowson for his work on the maps and plans, to Daniel Renton, Kim Reczek and Eleanor Bird for proof reading, and to all members of the GCDO and Butrint Foundation who provided photographs. Thanks too to Brian Donovan, Alket Islami and Tony Lumb for their photographs. Unless otherwise stated all photographs and illustrations are copyright of the GCDO/Butrint Foundation.

Photography title page: The Bazaar and castle *Left to right:* Palorto quarter and the Zekate House; Zekate House; Gjirokastra houses; The Ethnographic Museum *Left:* winter scene.

Welcome to Gjirokastra

"It was a strange town, and seemed to have been cast up in the valley one winter's night like some prehistoric creature that was now clawing its way up the mountainside. Everything in the city was old and made of stone, from the streets and fountains to the roofs of the sprawling age-old houses covered with grey slates like gigantic scales. It was hard to believe that under this powerful carapace the tender flesh of life survived and reproduced...

It was a steep city, perhaps the steepest in the world, defying the laws of architecture and city planning. The top of one house might graze the foundation of another, and it was surely the only place in the world where if you slipped and fell in the street, you might well land on the roof of a house - a peculiarity known most intimately to drunks."[1]

At first sight Gjirokastra appears extravagantly fanciful - an oriental vision of towering stone mansions clinging to the sheer sides of the valley. Dominated by a mighty limestone fortress that thrusts forward to accost those who approach along the valley, the city takes your breath away and you have to pinch yourself to be sure it is real. Once inside the old town, the steep network of cobblestone streets brings to mind the generations of people who have passed through these roads before - mountain warriors, imams, bustling traders, widows dressed in mourning black and Ottoman Turkish administrators with their beards and moustaches.

Old Gjirokastra is one of the best preserved examples of an Ottoman-style town in the Balkans and was inscribed as an UNESCO World Heritage Site in 2005. The city is known for its important contributions to Albanian culture and is the birthplace of many writers, artists and musicians, as well as Enver Hoxha, the notorious 20th century communist leader. Polyphonic singing, a hypnotic blend of harmonised voices, is traditional to the region. Much celebrated, it is performed widely, from public celebrations and weddings, to informal sessions in local cafés.

Left Looking northwest from the Castle
Above Gjirokastra Castle
Below Iso-polyphonic singers

A traditional stone roof

Gjirokastra is a modern city rooted faithfully in its past. Located on a spur of Mount Gjere approximately 300 m above sea level, the town holds a commanding position over the Drino Valley, which for thousands of years has been an important route linking the Adriatic to the East. The visitor can experience something of its turbulent history with a visit to its castle and its labyrinth of echoing galleries and tunnels, armaments museum and chilling Communist prison. In the old town you can wander round the cobbled bazaar, visit the Albanian Ethnographic Museum and experience what it was like to live in one of the dramatic fortified tower houses. A fascinating maze of tunnels built by the Communists as a nuclear shelter will soon be open to give visitors a taste of cold war paranoia, Albanian style. When you have finished exploring the cobbled streets and the curious tucked away corners of this historic mountainside city, you can slip into one of the many terraced bars to sip Turkish coffee and admire the spectacular views over the Drino Valley below.

Gjirokastra and the Drino Valley

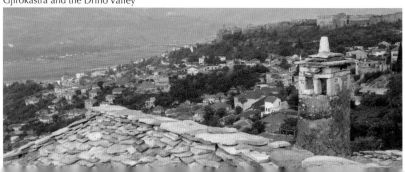

The countryside around Gjirokastra with its soaring mountains and deep river valleys offers plenty for the enterprising and curious traveller. You can take a tour to a remote village, climb a pass to spot eagles and rare butterflies, or visit one of many exceptional archaeological sites to explore the ancient history of the region.

This guidebook is designed to give you inspiration and help you enjoy your visit. The first two chapters provide historical information on Albania and Gjirokastra; the middle chapters consist of three walking tours around the city and castle, followed by a guide to visiting the main sites in the wider Gjirokastra region; and the final chapter contains practical information that will help you make the most of your stay.

A steep climb often leads to a great view

Whether you are visiting for a day, or staying longer in one of Gjirokastra's traditional bed and breakfasts, we hope this book will be an essential companion.

[1] Kadare, I., *Chronicle in Stone,* (Edinburgh: Serpent's Tail Publishing, 1987, pp. 1-2)

Bazaar Mosque

History of Albania

Skanderbeg statue, Skanderbeg Square, Tirana

Migrant populations, armies, travellers and traders have been crossing the Albanian landscape since it was first inhabited. This small country occupies a highly strategic position, a gateway between East and West, and its turbulent history is a story of invasion, occupation and perseverance.

The earliest urban centres were established in the 6th-5th centuries BC by the Illyrians, a mixed community of tribal peoples. Coastal areas were colonised by Greek settlers during this period and the ports of Apollonia and Dyrrhachium (Durrës) soon developed into important cities. A mingling of cultures is evident from subsequent settlements such as Byllis and Antigoneia, which have typically Illyrian hilltop locations coupled with Hellenistic architecture.

The Romans progressively infiltrated Illyrian territories, and by 167 BC, the region was under their control. In the 2nd century AD they began building one of the most important roads in Europe, the Via Egnatia, that ran from the Ionian port of Dyrrhachium east to Constantinople (Istanbul).

The origin of the modern name of the country can be found with the Arbers, also known as the Arbanitai or Albanoi, who inhabited the north of the region in the medieval period. In 1190, under the archon Progon, the fortified citadel of Kruja became the capital of the first Albanian feudal principality.

By the end of the 13th century, the region had been divided between Byzantines, Normans and Angevin French while other areas became part of the Despotate of Epirus. The 14th century saw invasion of the north by Serbs and then Venetians, and the growth of Albanian feudal kingdoms profiting from the warfare.

Right Kruja, Albania's first capital
Below Central Tirana, 1938

Ottoman Turks invaded from the south in 1385, and by 1417 controlled most of the Albanian territories. Even the fierce Albanian revolt of 1443 led by Gjergji Kastrioti (also known as Skanderbeg) could not halt their relentless progress. After Kastrioti's death in 1468, the Ottomans re-established themselves and ruled over Albania until 1912. Their quasi-feudal system of granting land in return for military dues allowed local governors to gain control of extensive areas. One of the most famous of these feudal lords, Ali Pasha of Tepelena, controlled southern Albania and Epirus from 1789 until his death in 1822.

The Albanian nation state was created on the 28th of November 1912 after the collapse of the Ottoman Empire. However, it was invaded by opposing armies during the First and Second World Wars with only a brief interwar independence under the premiership of Achmet Bej Zog, later King Zog. The Albanian Communist Party was formed in 1941 and initiated partisan warfare against the occupying Italian and German forces. Albania was finally liberated on the 29th of November 1944.

Top Tirana, 1928
Below Concrete bunkers in the Drino plain

Bazaar Mosque and roof tops

From 1944 to 1992 Enver Hoxha and his colleagues ruled Albania with a repressive Stalinist regime that became increasingly isolationist after the failure of successive international alliances. Hoxha imposed complete self-reliance on the country when China finally cut off aid in 1978. This caused rapid economic decline and culminated in economic and social collapse in the early 1990s. With the fall of the Communist Government in 1992, the population turned on the apparatus of their repression and what remained of the communist infrastructure was destroyed.

In the late 1990s, reconstruction began apace as Albania commenced transition to a free market. There was further unrest in 1997, but since then Albania has stabilised and become a growing economy with a European future.

Enver Hoxha and life in communist Albania

Enver Hoxha was born in Gjirokastra in 1908, the son of a prosperous cloth merchant. As a young man, he was strongly influenced by the growing spirit of nationalism that was the hallmark of early 20th-century Albania, and while studying in Korça, he discovered Marxism. He received a bursary from the Zogite Government to study at the University of Montpellier in France, but dropped out before completion. After a spell working in France and Belgium, he returned to Albania, teaching at Korça until the Italian invasion in 1939.

Hoxha was a founding member of the Albanian Communist Party in 1941, and he became its General Secretary in 1943. During the war he was one of the most influential leaders of the communist partisans based in the south of Albania, which proved to be an effective fighting force against the Nazis. The Albanian partisan resistance was fragmented and politically divided, but ultimately the allies accepted the predominance of Hoxha's communist National Liberation Committee over rival groups.

After the war, Hoxha became Albania's undisputed leader and modelled his government along Stalinist lines. He funded the industrial and agricultural development of the country through a series of alliances with Yugoslavia, the Soviet Union and China, all of whom invested heavily in Albania's infrastructure. It was Hoxha's brand of militant communism that put him at odds even with other hardline communist countries in the 1960s, and in 1961 he cut ties with the Soviet Union, and allied the country with China. A cultural revolution, Albanian style, followed, with the destruction of places of worship, and the widespread collectivization of private property. Dissenting voices or perceived opponents were violently repressed.

Top left Enver Hoxha at Mashkullora, March 1978 (*Enver Hoxha: His Life and Work*, Institute of Marxist Leninist Studies, Tirana, 1986) *Top right* Enver Hoxha's 1944 independence address (ibid)

Daily life was monotonous, frugal and intellectually restrictive. Everything from the length of a person's hair, to the use of (women's) make-up was carefully regulated and the ever-present security police - the Sigurimi - ensured that all dissent was efficiently quashed. Tens of thousands of political prisoners were placed in hard labour camps, and families without good *biografi* could expect to be penalised in all aspects of their daily lives.

However, this brand of communism brought benefits too. There was relative stability and Hoxha industrialised the country and brought electricity to the remotest regions. He emancipated women from a life of conservative drudgery and gave them equal status. He created jobs for the agrarian peasantry in newly built cities and factories, and he provided, for the first time, free education and health care to all citizens.

After the break with China, the country became increasingly isolated. Hoxha, paranoid with delusions that Albania would be invaded by Imperialists, Zionists and Socialist revisionists, spent his remaining years fortifying the country. Seven hundred thousand concrete bunkers were constructed to help repel invaders, millions of weapons were distributed in armouries across the countryside, and the population underwent extensive weapons training.

Isolation brought economic hardship and food shortages, and by the time of Hoxha's death in 1985, the country was ready for political change. Ramiz Alia, Hoxha's successor, attempted to liberalise Albania, but political events elsewhere in Europe soon overtook him. In 1990, the single party state was abandoned and in 1992, following widespread unrest, the Communist Government finally fell. This was the beginning of a chaotic decade of makeshift democracy and transition to a free market.

Communism in Albania was not a monolithic unchanging system and internal policy, which might be restrictive, militant or liberalised, reflected the international mood of communist policy.

Left Enver Hoxha's funeral 15th April 1985 (ibid) *Above* Ibrafim Shehu, *the phosphate refinery at Fier*

History of Gjirokastra

Archaeological evidence confirms that there has been a settlement at Gjirokastra for about 2500 years. Substantial block-built walls have been unearthed suggesting the site was a significant fortification in the pre-Roman period (before 168 BC), and probably refortified at the end of the Roman Empire. The first reference to the settlement was recorded in 1336 by the Byzantine chronicler John Cantacuzene.

The origin of the name Gjirokastra is less well defined. The most colourful suggestion is that it was named after Princess Argyro, the sister of the feudal lord of the town who threw herself from the battlements together with her young son during the final siege of the city by the Ottoman Turks. Given that the town's name appears in Byzantine records well before the Ottoman conquest, this is unlikely to be true. Another suggestion is that the name came from either the Argyres, a pre-Roman tribal group who inhabited the area. However, another more poetic explanation is that the city takes its name from the Greek word for silver, *argyros*, and is a reference to the grey stone walls, streets and slate roofs that shimmer like silver in the rain.

Below Ottoman-period tower houses

Hamam

Under the 13th-century Despotate of Epirus, the city and surrounding region were ruled by the Zenebishi family. The Ottoman Empire expanded into Europe in the late 14th century and Gjirokastra had fallen under its sway by 1419. The city prospered as part of the Ottoman Empire and it was the capital of the Albanian Sanjak (an Ottoman administrative unit) for over a century until it was superceded by Delvina during the reign of Sultan Suleiman the Magnificent (1520-1566). Gjirokastra retained an administrative role as the seat of a kadi (judge) and coupled with its strategic location and rich hinterland, the city remained important, and had doubled its pre-Ottoman population by 1583.

Ali Pasha of Tepelena took over the city in 1811 and it became a strategic and commercial stronghold between his twin capitals of Tepelena and Ioannina. He oversaw new fortification works including the construction of a 12 km aqueduct, which brought drinking water from Mount Sopot. The stone aqueduct was depicted by the British painter Edward Lear who travelled widely in the region. Its ruins were finally pulled down in 1932, but in the Manalat quarter a small section still

stands, known locally as Ali Pasha's Bridge or Manalat Bridge. After Ali Pasha was killed by the Sultan's forces, the city continued as an Ottoman administrative centre and as an agricultural and textile trading hub.

During the later part of the 19th century Gjirokastra was at the forefront of efforts to promote a sense of Albanian national identity. In 1880 the Assembly of Gjirokastra championed the cause of self-government and resistance to Ottoman rule. In 1908, Gjirokastra's first Albanian language school, named Liria, was opened in the city followed by a series of patriotic clubs and societies.

During the early 20th century Gjirokastra was a disputed territory as the frontiers of modern Albania were being defined. For a period following the collapse of Ottoman power and Albanian Independence in 1912, it formed part of the Autonomous Republic of Epirus under General Zographos who agitated for union with Greece.

Ali Pasha statue, Tepelena

After the First World War, the Entente powers (Great Britain, France and Russia) persuaded Greece to drop its claim to this majority ethnic Albanian area. The present frontier was ratified internationally in 1921.

During King Zog's reign (1928-1939), Gjirokastra established itself as one of the most important cultural and economic centres in the country, although it was also famous for the large prison constructed in the castle at this time. The city was taken by the Italians in 1939, provoking the formation of a guerrilla style resistance movement, known as the Partisans, who were opposed to the Italian and later German occupation. Much of the region was liberated in 1944 by the Partisans, and Gjirokastra became the base for the liberation of the rest of the country in November of the same year.

The years under communism saw extensive industrialisation. A metal-works factory made cutlery (occasionally you can see the remains of the stamped-out steel sheets used as garden fencing), and there were factories for shoes, clothing, cigarettes, umbrellas and other light industrial products. In 1961 Gjirokastra was declared a Museum City by the communist regime in an effort to conserve the unique cultural heritage of the town. A large workforce was assembled to maintain the old quarters.

When the regime fell in March 1992, Gjirokastra's economy was already declining rapidly. To achieve full employment, the communists had assigned far more people to work in the already outdated and inefficient industrial complexes than were actually required, and the subsequent collapse of communism resulted in the loss of thousands of jobs. There was much civil unrest, the National Armaments Museum was looted for weapons, and the enormous statue of Enver Hoxha that had dominated the old town for decades was pulled down.

There was further unrest in 1997 brought about by allegations of electoral fraud and the collapse of pyramid financial schemes that resulted in the loss of many people's life savings. A significant part of the Bazaar was burned and damaged, and the town became violent and lawless. The crisis triggered mass emigration, and the abandonment of many of the historic buildings that the state could no longer afford to maintain.

Today, Gjirokastra is reviving. The bulk of the local economy is based on agriculture, and businesses processing the region's high quality fruit, vegetables and dairy products are growing. The town is the administrative centre for the region and it has a well-attended university. The growth of tourism is the best hope for a vibrant economic future - an economy that should be sympathetic with the town's UNESCO status and unique cultural and architectural heritage.

Opposite View of Gjirokastra by Edward Lear, 1848 *Above* Remains of Ali Pasha's aqueduct, 1924 (Museum of Roman Civilization, Rome) *Below* Receiving alms during the Italian occupation, Second World War (A. Q. SH. i R. SH. Fototeka)

Çerçiz Topulli

Çerçiz Topulli was a resistance fighter of the early 20th century, and is considered a national symbol of exemplary courage and patriotism. Born in Gjirokastra in 1880, he was inspired by his older brother Bajo to become a fervent nationalist and left home as a young man to fight for Albanian independence. By 1907 he had become an outspoken activist and leader of a band of freedom fighters operating in the Gjirokastra and Korça regions.

Topulli achieved his status as a popular hero after a bloody period of fighting known as the War of Mashkullore, during which the Turks massacred the inhabitants of the village of Mashkullore just to the north of Gjirokastra, and left it to burn. The episode ended with a showdown in which the Bimbash, the Ottoman commander of the thousand-strong unit, was killed by Iso Labi, a member of Topulli's band. A stone plaque marks the exact spot on the Hazmurat Road leading down from the Neck of the Bazaar - see page 25.

Above Çerçiz Topulli and his band of freedom fighters (A. Q. SH. i R. SH. Fototeka) *Left* Çerçiz Topulli (A. Q. SH. i R. SH. Fototeka)

Çerçiz was held in high esteem by the Albanian people who would take great risks to protect him from the Ottoman authorities. One night Topulli and his band were surprised by a band of Turkish soldiers while sheltering in a teqe in Gjirokastra. The Babas dressed the freedom fighters as dervishes, the disguise made more convincing by the fighters' long beards. The Turks searched the premises, but duly left, their suspicions unaroused.

Albania achieved independence in 1912 and Topulli was killed three years later on the 15th of July 1915 near Shkodra in the north of the country while fighting off an invasion by Montenegro. In 1937 his body was transferred to Gjirokastra and the statue in the main square erected. He was named Hero of the People by the communist regime and in1947, his remains were exhumed and buried again in Gjirokastra's heroes' cemetery, with much ceremony, by Enver Hoxha.

Selam Musai and comrade by Hilmi Bani. Bani was another celebrated Southern Albanian freedom fighter

A guided walk of the Old Town

The city of Gjirokastra comprises the castle, the centre of the old town, the bazaar, and the historic residential quarters (Cfaka, Manalat, Dunavat, Teqe, Palorto, Varosh, Meçite, Hazmurat and Pllaka), which radiate out from the fortress. The new town, on the valley floor, is made up of mainly modern buildings as well as the university complex.

This guided walk will acquaint you with all the major sites of Gjirokastra's historic old town. The tour takes about three hours to complete, allowing you to stop briefly to take in the sites. For directions refer to the old town centre map in this chapter and the map on the inside front cover. Numbers on both these maps correspond to the numbers in the text below.

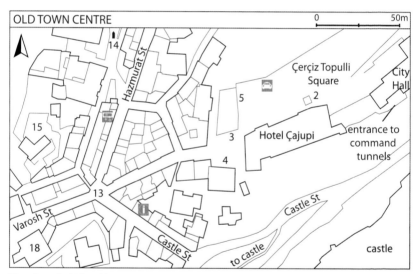

View from the Zekate House

1. Çerçiz Topulli Square

The walk begins in Çerçiz Topulli Square **(1)** the main square of the old town, which takes its name from the famous Albanian freedom fighter, a statue of whom stands at the edge of the square **(2)**. The monument, erected in 1934, was created by the great Albanian realist sculptor Odise Pascali, who is best known for his sculpture of the national hero Gjergji Kastrioti Skanderbeg in Tirana's Skanderbeg square. A small bullet hole in the right thigh of the Topulli statue was made by a drunk Italian officer during the Second World War, who decided to posthumously 'execute' the local hero.

There are several other monuments and features in Çerçiz Topulli Square:

Statue of Çerçiz Topulli

UNESCO Inscription (3)
This plaque commemorates the inscription of Gjirokastra as an UNESCO World Heritage Site in 2005.

UNESCO

The museum-City of Gjirokastra
was inscribed on the World Heritage List by the World Heritage Committee at its 29th session in July 2005 under the Convention Concerning the Protection of the World Cultural and Natural Heritage (UNESCO,1972)

Qyteti muze Gjirokastra
eshte perfshire ne Listen e Trashegimise Boterore nga Komiteti Boteror i Trashegimise ne mbledhjen e 29te te Korrikut 2005,ne Marreveshjen qe permbledh Mbrojtjen e Kultures Boterore dhe Trashegimine Natyrore (UNESCO,1972)

E. ÇABEJ   I. KADARE   M. KOKALARI

Monument to the Partisan Heroes

Monument to famous Gjirokastriotes (4)

To the right of the Çajupi Hotel there is a new monument built by the Municipality to celebrate three honorary citizens: Eqerem Çabej (1908-1980), an eminent historian, linguist and educator who was a founding member of the Albanian Academy of Sciences and gave his name to Gjirokastra University; Ismail Kadare (1936-), the internationally famous Albanian author; and Musine Kokalari (1917-1983), a writer and co-founder of the Albanian Social-Democratic Party (1943), who spent 37 years in prison during the communist regime and died, forsaken, in northern Albania.

Monument to the Partisan Heroes (5)

To the right of the tourist map there is a stone monument depicting two young women standing heroically with nooses around their necks. The Monument pays tribute to two teenage girls, Bule Naipi and Persefoni Kokëdhima, who were partisans during World War II, providing assistance to the rebel forces in the countryside. Betrayed to the German forces occupying the city, they were hanged in 1944.

National Folk Festival Sculpture (6)
Walk east through the square passing the Greek Consulate on your right. A little further, on the right, there is a large stone sculpture with a typical socialist-realist depiction of dancers and musicians in traditional costume. Designed by Ksenofon Kostaqi, it celebrates the National Folk Festival held in the city every four years. Above and to your right you will see the ruins of what was once the town's police station.

At this point, to your left, a narrow street passes parallel downhill. Take this route down to the Seven Fountains - a walk of about three minutes. The street is narrow with cars travelling in both directions. Be prepared to leap to the side to avoid oncoming vehicles.

Below National Folk Festival Sculpture

2. The Meçites Mosque, Seven Fountains and the Hamam

To your right, you will hear the sound of running water, which is the first of the Seven Fountains (7). The fountains were built into the foundations of the 17th century Meçites (meh-CHEET-ess) mosque, originally known as the mosque of Hadji Murad (Murad the Pilgrim). The remains of the minaret tower are immediately to the right of the fountain. A house now stands on the mosque's original foundations. The mosque, known for its fine decorated ceiling, was once reached by a stairway built over the fountains. Like many such religious buildings it was destroyed in 1967 during the Albanian Cultural Revolution (see page 52).

A few metres further, there is a path leading from the street to the right. Walk down the steps to see the remaining fountains, some of which are still in operation. The Muslim tradition is to purify oneself for prayer by washing and almost all mosques have a fountain or running water associated with them. The quantity of fountains here is perhaps exceptional and their building is recorded in a beautiful Ottoman inscription set over the central fountain:

Route down to Seven Fountains

"It has been constructed with a pool so as to be of great use.
Beginning from its base, to gain many prayers
The mosque shall be celebrated, so shall its founder be.
The one who built the pool shall be happy
From all believers, to this pool and to its builder
Since Muin Arslan is the naib and owner of the word.
For me today, tomorrow for you, (even) prophets have passed away.
With kindness, with pure sincerity, grant proper prayer to all."

Return to the road and turn right around the corner on the path to get the best view of the Hamam **(8)**, a traditional Turkish bathhouse with a double domed roof. The building comprises an entrance courtyard, a block of heated rooms with three domed chambers and other rooms. As was common with southern Albanian-style baths the domes are roofed with the traditional grey slate and this is a good opportunity to examine the skill of the construction. The Hamam has recently been restored by the Gjirokastra Conservation and Development Organization but is currently not open to visitors.

Returning to the street, turn right and continue for a few minutes until you reach an intersection and the Rruga Hazmurat. The renovated Orthodox seminary **(9)** is on the right and a war memorial diagonally opposite. Turn left and walk up the hill into the Bazaar.

After about 100 m there is a plaque on the right set into the stone wall depicting the image of a pistol. It commemorates the assassination of the Turkish Bimbash by Iso Labi in 1908 (see page 18) **(10).** A little further on to the left is another stone plaque commemorating Dule Muço, who in 1944 at the age of 15 killed several Nazis with a Molotov cocktail **(11)**.

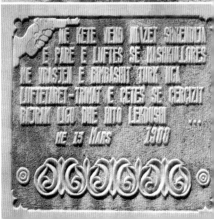

Top One of the Seven Fountains
Middle Hamam
Bottom Plaque commemorating the assassination of the Turkish Bimbash

3. The Bazaar

Life in Gjirokastra has long centred around the medieval castle, and many of the inhabitants once lived inside its stout walls. In pre-Ottoman times, the population would have relied on trade, while some served the feudal lords, the Zenebishi clan, who controlled the region and used the castle as their base. The Zenebishi were one of a number of families competing to control the remains of the Despotate of Epirus, a Byzantine successor-state long-established in the area.

As the Ottomans consolidated their conquests in the region they made Gjirokastra the capital of the new Albanian sanjack (province) which they established in 1419. The growing administration and the supporting garrison provided the stimulus for the town to expand. Initially it was concentrated on the east slope outside the castle gate, an area still known as the Pazari i Vjetër (Old Bazaar) **(12)**.

Above Pazari i Vjetër

In the 1430s, Ottoman records listed 163 dwellings. By the 1580s the town had more than 400 dwellings, and Gjirokastra had become a trading centre to complement its administrative importance. In the 17th century, Memi Pasha, the Ottoman governor, planned and built a new commercial centre for Gjirokastra along the northern slope of the hill, the Pazari i Ri (New Bazaar, referred to hereafter simply as the Bazaar) **(13)**. The new quarter, which included a mosque, dwellings and shops, was almost completely destroyed by fire in the 18th century. It was rebuilt in the 1750s and again in 1912. What you see today dates from that reconstruction. Typically each of the two-storey premises has a shop or workshop below and living space above. This simple design has been much altered over the centuries and many now have rambling extensions at the back.

The Hani Zagoria (Zagoria Inn) on Rruga Hazmurat is a recently restored example.

Fantazia view (14)
Walk up the black cobblestone road until you see a ramp on the right heading upwards. Follow the ramp (watch out for cars coming from both directions) and bear left as the path forks.

The wide paved area in front of you, which now serves as a car park, was once the location of an enormous statue of Enver Hoxha that watched over the city. There are spectacular views of the town from here - notice how you can clearly see the division of the old town from the new, the slate gabled roofs above and the flat concrete roofs below.

Below View from the Fantazia restaurant

The Obelisk (15)

Head back down the ramp and continue along the narrow street that runs past the Raifeissen Bank (which has an ATM). Walk past the dilapidated shop fronts and past the street on your left that leads back to the centre of the Bazaar, known as the Neck. A little further on, to your right, walk through a double wooden door (if it's locked, ask for the key at the Tourist Information Centre), and climb the stone stairs to emerge onto a wide terrace with a large obelisk in the middle.

This monument, called Mëmëdheu ABC, pays tribute to Albanian education in the 20th century. There are breathtaking views of the city from here, especially of the historic neighbourhoods of Varosh (below), Palorto (the hill towards the right) and Dunavat (higher on the hill towards the left).

The Obelisk was built adjacent to the site of the first Albanian language school, which opened in Gjirokastra in 1908. During the Ottoman occupation, the teaching of the native language was forbidden, and despite the slow collapse of the Ottoman Empire, the construction of the school demonstrated defiance and courage. It reflected both the growing sense of Albanian national identity, as well as a typically Gjirokastriote spirit of rebellion. Nevertheless, the teachers who work there risked imprisonment and persecution. This is also where Eqerem Çabej, one of Gjirokastra's most remarkable sons, used to live (see p. 22). Today the building houses the Gjirokastra Conservation and Development Organization.

Go back down to the street, turn left and take the short road on the right. This leads directly into the Neck of the Bazaar.

The Obelisk

Castle Street

Neck of the Bazaar (13)

The Qafë (CHA-fuh) or Neck of the Bazaar is the busy intersection of five streets that forms the heart of the old town. In the mornings and evenings it throngs with people as the men of the old town take their twice-daily promenades and have coffee in one of the many street cafés. Your visit to Gjirokastra will take you through here many times, but it is worth stopping for a while, perhaps at a café, to take it all in. Don't be surprised if someone tries to engage you in conversation. The Bazaar regulars are quite friendly and speak enough English (or Italian, French, Greek, even Russian) for a brief chat.

Walk up Castle Street towards the castle. When you pass the Tourist Information Centre on your left, call in and ask them to check that Saint Sotira Church, the Ethnographic Museum

and the Zekate House will all be open later. If they are closed, the Centre can call to arrange different times for you. Pick up an information leaflet for the Ethnographic Museum here.

Bazaar

4. Saint Sotira Orthodox Church (16)
Open daily 0700 to 0730
and 1900 to 1930
Sunday services are from 0700 to 1000
Free admission

Saint Sotira is located at the northeast end of the castle mount. To get there, continue up Castle Street and follow the road to the left as it leads up and along the base of the castle. It can be steep in places. Passing a spur that leads up to the main gate of the castle, continue north eastwards until you pass the path leading up to the north gate. Take the road down through the Pllaka quarter, which used to be the town's bazaar until the 17th century. Saint Sotira Church is about 200 m along this road on the left-hand side. Walk down the narrow path marked by a glass case containing an icon and turn right through a gate into the small courtyard. The entrance is on the left. If you would prefer to take a taxi you will need to return to the taxi rank in Çerçiz Topulli Square.

The church was built in 1784 and is of a typical Orthodox design - rectangular in shape and built on an east-west axis. Worshippers enter by the west end, symbolizing the entrance of the faithful from the darkness of sin (the west) into the light of truth (the east). The church is also called the Old Metropolitan, as it was once the seat of the local Orthodox bishop. Today the Albanian Orthodox Church is autocephalous, meaning it is independent of the Eastern Orthodox Church's authority in Istanbul.

All Orthodox churches are built to represent the universe and symbolise the meeting point between heaven and earth. The ceiling represents heaven and the floor represents the mundane world. Saint Sotira's domed ceiling has an icon of Christ Pantocrator, the all-ruling Christ, looking down from heaven upon the assembled congregation, hearing their prayers and reminding them of his omnipresence. The altar is raised from the floor and accessed by a series of steps, symbolising a meeting point between heaven and earth.

Just inside the church and to the right is the metamorphosis, a hand-carved stand holding two icons that symbolises the divine transformation of Christ. Upon entering, the faithful cross themselves, bow three times and then kiss the icon. To the left of the entrance is a table holding candles. It is customary to make a donation (the slot is on the left end of the table) and take the candle to one of the brass stands, saying a prayer for someone as you light it.

The interior of the church was heavily damaged during communism and the original wall paintings have been destroyed. Framed icons now cover the walls, many of them painted recently by local artists.

The church is divided into three main parts. The two-tiered area at the back of the church where you enter is called the narthex and was originally the place where unbaptised or non-Orthodox congregation stood during services. The nave is divided by two rows of three large columns. The ornate chair was originally intended for the local Orthodox bishop. The objects hanging from the steel bars, called censers, hold incense or candles (the three chains symbolizing the Holy Trinity). Some of these were rescued from other churches during the period of communist destruction.

The third part of the church is the sanctuary, divided from the nave by the ornately carved iconostasis. This beautiful two-tiered screen dates from the late 18th century. All the small icons along the top tier are original as are the two icons on either side of the central, or royal, door on the lower tier. All the remaining icons along the lower tier are replacements, as is the cross at the centre top of the iconostasis, the originals having been stolen during the communist years. The icons depict Christ, Mary and various saints and are symbolic of the holy gathering around Christ's throne, represented by the altar inside the sanctuary. Another purpose of the iconostasis is to restrict entry into the sanctuary, which is off-limits to people who are not consecrated officials of the Orthodox Church.

Below Saint Sotira church

5. The Medresa and Mosque

Retrace your steps back past the castle, bearing right down the hill toward the Bazaar, but continue straight ahead rather than taking the right turn that takes you to the Neck. You will pass the town's only public conveniences on the left. Across the street you will see a yellow building with a domed roof that looks a bit like a mosque. This two-storey octagonal building, constructed in 1727, used to be a Bektashi teqe and was closed down during the communist period. Today it is a medresa, or Islamic school **(17)**.

The Medresa is open to boys aged between 14 and 18 years old and has an intake of 50-60 students per year. It is the equivalent of the Albanian shkolla e mesme (high school).

In addition to the standard high school curriculum of maths, sciences, Albanian language, literature and English language, there is a religious component that includes learning Arabic, Islamic history, and the study, reading and singing of the Qur'an. Students also receive some instruction in the Turkish language as the school is sponsored by a Turkish non-governmental organisation.

Across the road from the Medresa is the fine, but sadly dilapidated Babameto House dating to 1887. A little past the Medresa on the same side of the street is a staircase leading down, which can be followed to reach the road below. You are now facing Gjirokastra's only active mosque.

Above Medresa *Right* Bazaar Mosque

The Mosque (18)
Open daily
Free admission

The Imam is happy to welcome tourists. The best time to visit is about 15 minutes after one of the five daily prayer times (dawn, noon, mid-afternoon, sunset, night-time), when prayers are finished and the Imam is certain to be present.

There were once 15 mosques in Gjirokastra, 13 of which survived until the communist religious persecutions reached their climax in 1967, when 12 were destroyed. No one knows why this particular mosque was spared, although some believe its status as a cultural monument must have saved it. After 1967 the building, with its high domed ceiling, was used to train circus acrobats. Since the end of the communist regime, the mosque has been reinstated. It remains a place of both religious and social significance, where people from around the town meet for prayer and to discuss social and community issues.

The Mosque was part of Memi Pasha's original 17th-century plan for the Bazaar. It was destroyed by a fire in the 18th century, and was rebuilt around 1757 along with the rest of the Bazaar. The Mosque was deliberately designed to extend over the original street front, creating a small parade of enclosed shops that were rented out to provide funds for its maintenance.

On the west side of the building at street level is a small octagonal building that is used for the ritual washing of hands and feet before the faithful attend prayers inside the Mosque. The front doors of the Mosque have carved Arabic inscriptions: the one on the right invokes Allah; the one on the left the Prophet Muhammad, founder of Islam. The room inside the main doors is the men's prayer room. Women pray separately from men in a prayer room to the left of the main entrance. The wall opposite the door faces towards Mecca and it is from here that the Imam leads worship. Known as the qibla, it contains a sacred niche (mihrab) that forms the focus of prayer. The small set of stairs (minbar) to the right is where the Imam stands to deliver his weekly message during the mid-day Friday prayers.

In his message he stresses devotion to God and the avoidance of vices. The uppermost platform is reserved for the Prophet and is never used by the Imam.

In the corner to the right of the main entrance is the entrance to the minaret tower. There are 99 steps to reach the top, each symbolising the names of God as given in the Qur'an. The tower was built with stones that each had a hole drilled through the centre.

Once they were stacked in place, the holes aligned and molten lead was poured through the stones to help seat and consolidate the blocks. Before amplification systems became the norm, the call for prayer was sung from the top of the minaret five times each day. These days, bats are now said to be the only occupants of the minaret, and the call is issued via the microphone inside the main prayer room.

7. Ethnographic Museum (19)
Open daily April to September 0800 to 1200 and 1600 to 1900
October to March Wednesday to Sunday 0800 to 1600
Admission: Lek 200

To get to the Ethnographic Museum, turn left onto the black-cobbled road running past the Mosque, and walk westward towards the large regional council building called the Qarku, (Ch-arku) **(20)**.

Turn left immediately after the Qarku and the Ethnographic Museum is about 100 m ahead. You are now in the Palorto quarter where many of the largest and grandest traditional houses are found.

Gjirokastra's Ethnographic Museum stands on the site of the childhood home of Enver Hoxha, Albania's communist dictator from 1944 to 1985.

Above Ethnographic Museum
Right Ethnographic Museum interiors

The museum building was constructed in 1966, after the original house was destroyed by fire. It is modelled on a traditional Gjirokastra house with many of the classic cultural elements. From 1966 to 1991 the building served as the National Liberation War Museum. In 1991 the exhibits from the previous Ethnographic Museum were moved into this space. There are four floors, exhibiting household items, folk costumes and cultural artefacts typical of a wealthy 19th-century Gjirokastra family of merchants or Ottoman administrators. The rooms are laid out as they would have been, and give a sense of the very comfortable lifestyle such a house provided. The Tourist Information Centre can provide a leaflet giving details of the museum contents.

8. Zekate House (21)

No set opening hours - ask in the
Tourist Information Centre
Admission: €1.00

There are two ways to get to the Zekate
House, one of the uppermost dwellings
in the town. The longer but less taxing
route is to walk back along the road
that you used to get to the Ethnographic
Museum, taking the fork to the right
just past the kindergarten (which sports
a colourful sign). There is a set of steps
immediately on the right going up.
Take the steps and follow the road up
past the Kalemi Hotel, until you reach
the Zekate House.

The second and more direct route is
up a small road, Rruga Reshat Zani,
just before the Ethnographic Museum.
The road is very steep, and if the white
limestone surface is wet this route is
slippery (see page 88). The Zekate
House faces you at the top of the road.
This was the original approach to the
building and the disused gate at the
head of this path was the main guest
entrance. The new entrance gate is
reached by walking left along the front
of the house to the road leading up
from the south. If you took the gentler
route passing the Kalemi Hotel you will
arrive directly at the new entrance.

Initially you enter the courtyard of the
neighbouring house, where the owners
of the Zekate House now live. They
will take you into the house or provide
you with the keys, after collecting the
admission fee. The Zekate House
is unoccupied.

This particularly grand fortified tower
house was constructed in 1811-1812
with twin towers and a great double-
arched façade. The two arches,
kamerie, were erected for structural
reasons, but demonstrate the
extraordinary grandeur of the four-
storeyed buiding. The owner and
builder of the house was Beqir Zeko,
a general administrator in Ali Pasha's
government and the house reflects his
status within the ruling elite of the
town. Zeko shared the house with his
sons and their families.

Above Zekate House

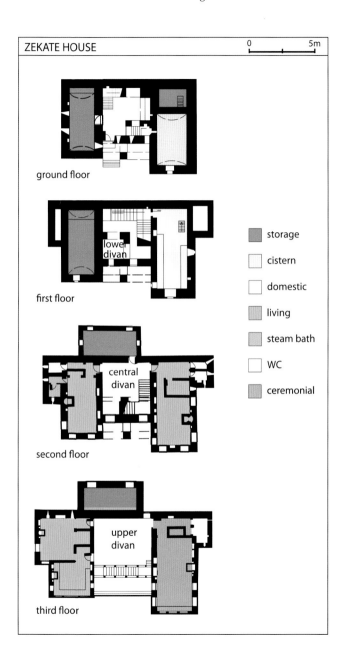

ZEKATE HOUSE

0   5m

ground floor

first floor

lower divan

second floor

central divan

third floor

upper divan

storage
cistern
domestic
living
steam bath
WC
ceremonial

Zekate House interior

used by the women of the household. Situated directly over the cistern it was cool and had a dedicated under-floor storage area for food. Cooking facilities were also located here.

The second floor contains two main rooms leading off from the central divan. Similar in layout, they were used by the two branches of the family as winter rooms, as their stone walls made them easier to heat. Each has an adjacent toilet and bathroom (hamam), which were heated by the fires in the main rooms. Low couches ran around three sides of the rooms and storage cupboards are built into the walls. At one end is the musandra, a large cupboard, which stored mattresses and other bedding during the day.

The musandra conceals a short staircase leading to a small gallery overlooking each room. Women and children retired to these galleries during formal meetings when the men of the house received guests.

The third floor, the uppermost timber gallery, contains the grandest reception room as well as two smaller rooms. The walls are wooden lath covered with a special plaster compound produced from a mix of aged lime, goat hair, egg whites, fine sand, mixed with straw. The third floor divan is especially grand with a spectacular view over the town and valley below. The head of the family and his chief guests would have sat on the raised dais to drink coffee and smoke. The two smaller rooms are summer chambers following the model of the rooms on the floor below.

The imposing front door leads into a lower hallway. To the right is a large water cistern lined with plaster. The status of a house was to some degree measured by the capacity of its cistern. The first autumn rains would be permitted to clean off the roof and thereafter the extensive guttering would direct the fresh supplies into the cistern below. To the left of the front door is a large vaulted storeroom for milling cereals.

The staircase that winds through the centre of the building is paved with grey slates outlined in a red paint that protects the soluble lime cement from being washed away by frequent cleaning.

The first floor contains the lower divan or reception chamber and has a small raised section in one corner where important people sat. There is one separate room on this level that was

The principal room on this floor was intended to be a multipurpose reception room. It is large and elaborately decorated and was used for the most important social occasions. The fresco decoration of garlands of fruit and flowers is very typical of the "Tulip Period" of Ottoman architectural design, and has symbolic meanings for the health, wealth and abundance of the household. The design and decoration of the house is thought to be the work of the master architect and decorator, Petro Korcare, who was a favourite of Ali Pasha.

An elaborate gallery and musandra covers the entrance door and adjacent toilet. The ceiling is very finely carved, and gilded. The windows, bar the lunettes with their multicoloured glass, are unglazed to allow a cooling draft.

9. Return to the Bazaar

From the Zekate House, you have the pleasure of knowing that the trip back to the Bazaar, or nearly anywhere else in Gjirokastra, is all downhill! The Bazaar has many places to eat and drink and the walk down takes about 15 minutes. However, for an even better view walk *up* the road for 15 minutes and have lunch at the restaurant on Kerculla Rock **(22)**.

Palorto quarter and the Zekate House

Gjirokastra's fortified tower houses

Angonates, Gjirokastra's largest house

Relaying a roof with limestone tiles

Gjirokastra's great glory is its fortified tower houses, known as kullë (tower), which symbolise the wealth and prestige of the city from the 17th century onwards. Most were built in the 18th and 19th centuries during the Ottoman occupation, and belonged to wealthy individuals such as administrative officials or merchants. Although broadly Ottoman in style, the Gjirokastra tower houses are a unique blend of Ottoman and local architectural elements. An important feature is the general lack of a distinct division between selimlik (male) and haremlik (female) quarters, which is characteristic of all other Ottoman houses.

The local topography has also helped shape the houses: on a sharp gradient, it is easier to build up than across, and the steep banks behind the houses negate the need for extensive scaffolding. Although the houses appear fortified with defensive embrasures set in the walls, much of this is for show. In reality, the hill is often so close to the back of the house, window access is possible with just a short plank.

The houses typically consist of a lower stone block, often several storeys high, topped by a wooden gallery with several large rooms to house an extended family. Each house has a yard containing smaller buildings, known as odajashta (external rooms). These were often used for cooking, but many were later converted for other uses.

Sadly many of these houses have fallen into serious disrepair. Due to emigration, the high cost of maintenance, and the relative inaccessibility of the old town, a great number now stand empty. During communist times the buildings were cared for, but now there is a diminishing pool of skilled labour capable of restoring the buildings to their former glory. However, in 2008, a programme began to train new specialists in conservation and work is ongoing to restore the most significant historic houses. In the meantime, visitors can still get a feel for the grandeur of Gjirokastra's past with a wander through the quarters of Dunavat, Manalat, and Palorto. A few of the most important houses are listed here:

The Angonates House lies on the road above the Ethnographic Museum (**19**)*. It is the largest of all the Gjirokastra houses and dates back to the 18th century, although after changing hands it was completely reconstructed in 1838 to form the elaborate two-storey mansion we can see today. The older part of the house is at the southern end while the northern extension includes a large water cistern, a feature of many Gjirokastra houses.

The Babameto House is an elegant two-storey building across the road from the medresa (**17**). It is unusual in that it was built to appear as one house, while in reality it is two - an interesting solution to the problem of housing an extended family. With a well nearby, the house had no need for a cistern, which may have seemed an expensive luxury.

In Varosh Street, where the main post office can be found, there are a number of fine buildings. Off to the northern side of the road situated in an alley, there is a complex originally belonging to the Fico family. One 18th-century building is cleverly extended by terracing up the slope, and next to it stands the last kullë built in Gjirokastra in 1902. Representing a fusion of old with new, the exterior, although grand, is far less decorative than earlier buildings, and internally it is much simpler. There are fewer rooms with inbuilt musandra (cupboards) to store bedding, indicating the arrival of western-style furniture and separate apartments for bedrooms. European ideas, and even American imports brought back by returning emigrants, were beginning to affect the architectural and interior design.

Numbers in this section refer to the map inside the front cover

The ornately decorated Fico House

Restoration of the Gurgai House

The Xheneti House

Gjirokastra Castle

Archaeologists believe that the site of Gjirokastra Castle has been inhabited since the Iron Age in the 8th - 7th centuries BC. The first fortifications were probably erected from the 5th century BC during the time when Epirus was a battle-ground between Illyrian tribes, Macedonians and the forces of Rome. A much larger fortress, eventually occupying an area of 2.5 ha, was built on the eastern end of the ridge overlooking the valley by the Despotate of Epirus under Byzantine auspices in the 12th and 13th centuries. After the decline of the Byzantine Empire, the region around Gjirokastra was ruled by the Albanian Zenebishi clan, who occupied the castle prior to the Ottoman invasion.

After the Ottoman conquest of the late 14th century, the castle was progressively enlarged and improved. The first extensive additions are believed to have been made around 1490 by Sultan Beyazid II, who also built a mosque inside the walls. Extensions were built throughout the Ottoman period as the castle grew south westward down the ridge. Little remains of these early phases except for some sections of the outer walls and towers, and a few sections of masonry exposed in the galleries during archaeological excavations.

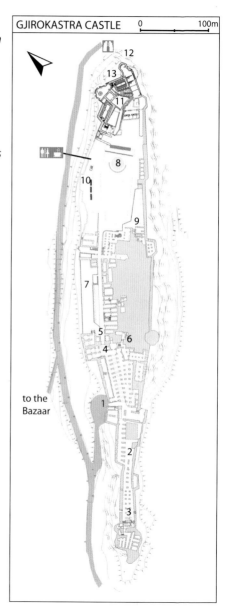

GJIROKASTRA CASTLE   0   100m

to the
Bazaar

From 1811, the Ottoman governor Ali Pasha of Tepelena embarked on a substantial building programme, adding the clock tower at the eastern end, and completing the western fortifications to enclose the full area now occupied by the castle. He also built an aqueduct to bring water down a distance of about 10 km from a spring under Mount Sopot to fill the massive water cisterns that lie in the central block of the castle. Ali Pasha's ambitions to fortify his dominions sufficiently to be able to rebel against the Ottoman Sultan came to nothing when the Sultan overthrew and executed him in 1822. Since Ali Pasha's day, the fortunes of the castle have slowly declined. What was left of the aqueduct was torn down in the early 1930s and the stones used to construct a prison in the heart of the fortress that remained in use for over 30 years.

Castle guided walk
Open daily April to September
0900 to1900
October to March 0900 to1700
Castle Admission: Lek 200
National Armaments Museum
Admission: Lek 200

Numbers in this chapter correspond to the castle plan to the left.

Main gate (1)

To reach the main gate from the Neck of the Bazaar walk up Castle Street turning right at the second junction, and finally left up to the gate. Alternatively there is a very steep, but more direct, path up the hillside from Castle Street. There is a small parking area in front of the main gate. The guard at the gate will sell you a ticket for the castle.

Below Castle and Old Bazaar

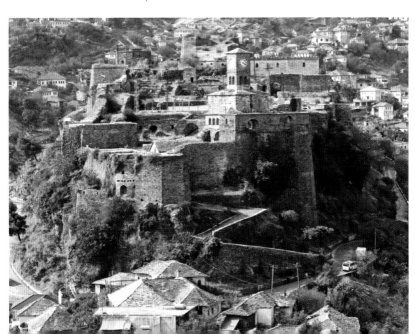

Remains of the aqueduct, known as the Manalat Bridge

Bektashi turbe (2)

Once through the main gate, follow the vaulted corridor and turn right into the main gallery. Pause to look at the huge space of the Vezir's Gate on the left. This was one of the principal gates to the castle leading down and to the south. Its fine stonework includes denticluated mouldings and the remains of a second storey including the vault, doors, stairs and chimney breasts. A number of the internal spaces in the castle held second and third floors acting as the residences for the castle's officials and its garrison. Return to the main path and follow this to the left (be cautious, it is often slippery) for about 50 m along the vaulted gallery. You will pass a still-functioning cistern, part of Gjirokastra's mains water supply. On the left, up some steps, you will see a small house tucked into the walls of the castle, surrounded by a small garden. This is a Bektashi turbe, or tomb. It contains the remains of two Bektashi Fathers, Baba Sulltan and Baba Kapllan, holy men of the 16th-17th century who lived and worked in Gjirokastra.

The vaults of Ali Pasha (3)

Continuing to the west of the turbe it is possible to navigate through a series of tunnels and massive vaults to the very western tip of the castle. These substructures and the fortifications above were constructed by Ali Pasha after 1811. They form the foundations of the ramparts above and also served as storehouses and guardrooms. Considerable engineering skills were employed here, as in other similar underground vaults and chambers all over the castle, and it was once possible to walk underground from one end of the castle to the other. It is believed that Ali Pasha used a German military engineer to design the complex after falling out with Pietro Korcari, his Albanian architect. These passages are dark, difficult underfoot and damp. Visitors are advised that they proceed at their own risk and if you intend to undertake the exploration you must bring a good torch as there is virtually no natural light. To continue the tour, retrace your steps to the main entrance.

Great Gallery, artillery and the tank (4)
Turning left from the main entrance **(1)** enter a long gallery that widens out into a substantial vaulted space. A parallel gallery that runs along the eastern side can be viewed through the windows and doorways to the left. This contains a section of the medieval castle's wall exposed during archaeological excavations. With a completely different alignment to the present building it is clearly from an earlier structure.

The Great Gallery is lined with artillery pieces. These guns were either abandoned by or captured from the Italian and German occupation forces during World War II. Italian guns, with a few exceptions, occupy the right side of the gallery. Several are of Austro-Hungarian origin, and were delivered to the Italians as war reparations after World War I. German artillery lines the left side of the gallery. At the end of this gallery on the left is a small Italian tank. Built by Fiat from 1941 to 1943, the L6/40 had a 20mm main gun and a two-man crew. Only 283 of these tanks were ever produced. Adjacent is a copy of the massive statue of the Partisan Hero by Odise Paskali, who also made the sculpture of Çerçiz Topulli in the main square.

Albanian National Armaments Museum (6)
Just beyond the Italian tank on the left is the door to the ticket office for the Albanian National Armaments Museum **(5)**. Usually the maroon-uniformed security guard will take you here when you enter through the main entrance.

Originally opened in 1971, the Albanian National Armaments Museum is located in what was once part of the prison. There are two main galleries that trace the history of Albanian conflict from the later 19th century independence movements up until the Second World War. On display are Albanian arms used during the independence struggles of 1912 and 1920 as well as arms used by Albanian Partisans, and trophies from World War II. Most of the museum is dedicated to the Partisan struggle against the Italian and German occupation forces from 1939 to 1944.

Above The main gallery
Below Flat L6/40 tankette

The room devoted to the Second World War has as its centre piece a copy of an Odise Paskali sculpture of a partisan beating down the Nazi enemy. The original stands at Mauthausen concentration camp in Austria. A great array of captured German and Italian arms are on display including some rare pieces such as the Sturmgewher 44, the first true assault rifle, and the weapons of the Partisans including many British-manufactured guns provided as military aid. There is also a fine selection of Albanian socialist realist paintings throughout the museum.

Right First World War 75mm field gun

The prison (6)
Entrance to the prison is gained through a set of open steel doors in the first gallery of the National Armaments Museum. Designed by the Italians, the prison was built by King Zog's regime and used from 1932.

It was taken over by the Italian and German occupation forces during the Second World War, then by the communist regime in 1944, and finally closed in 1968. Until the early1960s it was the largest of the many Albanian prisons used by the communist regime to punish dissidents.

The small part of the prison that is accessible to visitors was developed as a museum by the communist regime in the 1970s following the model of 'revolutionary' jails in the Soviet Union and elsewhere. The writing on the walls and the pen-and-ink drawings depict the exploits of communist heroes who were confined here during Zog's rule and the occupations of Second World War. The writings include newspaper articles and prisoners' diary entries. Unfortunately there are no translations currently available, but the cold and forbidding atmosphere is quite enough to give you a feel for the horrors perpetrated here.

Left Prison cell

At the far end of the cellblock, adjacent to a torture and execution chamber, is a macabre display commemorating the young girl partisans, Bule Naipi and Persefoni Kokëdhima, who were executed in the prison. The display case contains the girls' clothing and the rope that is purported to be the one used for their hanging by the Nazis in 1944.

At the far end of the corridor, through the locked steel bars to the right, you can see the rest of the prison and the punishment cells. Since it was closed, the area has been used as a film set, which accounts for the paint scheme.

Above Communist-era print of prison escape
Left Prison exercise yard *Top* Prison corridor

The American aeroplane and antique cannon collection (7)

Return through the Armaments Museum and go out onto the ramparts passing the ticket office on your left. You will see ahead of you the remains of a United States Air Force two-seat trainer, a Lockheed T-33 Shooting Star. The aeroplane was forced to land at Rinas Airport, near Tirana in December 1957, after developing technical problems. The plane was further damaged upon landing because of the poor runway surface. The pilot was returned to the United States a short time later, but the plane was retained by the Albanian authorities. This proud trophy of the Cold War, which the communist regime maintained was a spy plane, was brought to the castle in 1969.

Nearby there is a collection of antique cannon. These are the remains of the original Ottoman fortress guns, and many of them date from the time of Ali Pasha. Ottoman policy was to keep the military arsenal available to local governors to a minimum, and so castles and fortresses tended to be equipped with ancient artillery, sometimes centuries out of date. This collection is typical, ranging from two- to 12-pounder guns. Many of them are naval weapons, removed from ships. The large wide-mouthed carronade is one example, a characteristic weapon of warships in the 19th century. A number of these pieces, and others in the castle, are old British-cast guns, remnants of the military aid given to the Ottoman Empire by their long-term allies the British. The nine pounder gun at the entrance to the Armaments Museum was presented to Ali Pasha in 1810, along with other supplies by the British diplomat and spy William Martin Leake.

Left Emerging onto the ramparts
Below Cannon and the captured US plane

Festival stage (8)

The stage was erected in the 1980s and has for some years been the home of the Albanian National Folk Festival, held every four years (the last one was in 2008). During the year the stage is used by the Municipality to present, amongst other events, music and dancing on public holidays such as Liberation Day and Independence Day.

The castle ramparts (9)

It is not advisable to explore the south side of the castle to the east of the prison. There are no barriers or other warnings of hazards such as crumbling walls or concealed holes. The series of cathedral-sized cisterns were built under this area by Ali Pasha and supplied from the west by the aqueduct. Their entrances are high up in the south walls.

Views to the north (10)

There are spectacular views of the town and surrounding mountains from all along the north wall of the castle.

Above Castle battlements
Below Castle from Dunavat quarter

Clock tower (11)

The clock tower was erected by Ali Pasha in the 19th century and dominates the east end of the castle. Determining the time of the five daily prayers is an important part of the Muslim day. The Ottomans had a rich culture of clock making and from the 17th century onwards they built clock towers right across their Empire. The square tower of the Gjirokastra clock is a typical example.

The original clock worked on a counterbalance system: a winch on the tower floor was used to raise several cylindrical weights which slowly descended through the hole in the floor, thereby moving the clock hands. The original bell was allegedly stolen by one of the foreign occupying armies during the Second World War. The current tower is a 1980s restoration and the clock, installed in the 1990s, is in need of repair.

The bastion

Below the clock tower is a large vaulted bastion once the site of a battery of cannon. The embrasures dominate both the town and the approach road to the main castle gates. Nearby, down a stone staircase, is the rectangular powder store, carefully isolated from the surrounding ground surface by a vaulted passage.

Views to the east (12)

The extreme eastern end of the castle is a wonderful spot to view the picturesque Drino River and Valley. From here Mount Cajupi dominates the horizon, and the villages on its lower slopes, including the site of the ancient city of Antigoneia, can be seen with binoculars. Please take care, there are some steep drops with no safety barriers and caution is needed, especially with children.

Top left Clock tower
Top right Stepped path down to the East Gate

East gate (13)

In between the clock tower and the eastern edge of the castle is a steep, winding path that leads to the east gate. The path is specially stepped for caravans of pack animals, who would have formed the main means of transport when the castle was built.

Normally this gate is locked. If by chance it is open, you can exit here, otherwise retrace your steps to the main gate to complete the tour.

Above Northeast bastion
Below Gjirokastra at night

Mosques and teqes in Gjirokastra

Many of Gjirokastra's Islamic buildings survived until the 20th century, and early photographs show the cityscape studded with minarets. However, between 1966-68, Enver Hoxha launched a nationwide campaign of desecration as part of the "Albanian Cultural Revolution"; almost all religious buildings were torn down or converted to a secular use - often as armouries or store rooms. Mosques were a particular target as their minarets were so visible. This campaign was implemented with particular vigour in Gjirokastra; as it was Enver Hoxha's birth place and

central to his personality cult, no rivals to his pre-eminence could be permitted.

Nevertheless, some remains of mosques and teqes can still be seen today. The Madresa behind the bazaar mosque was once the focus of a Bektashi teqe, and a fine domed mosque, minus its minaret, still survives in the Dunavat quarter (see p. 57). The old town guided walk takes you to the Meçites Mosque and its attendant fountain and hamam complex (see p. 24), while on the hill above the Eqerem Çabei University on the far side of the new town, lies the recently reoccupied Bektashi teqe **(23)***.

Dating from the 17th century or before, the Teqeja e Kodrës së Shtufit (Hill of Tuff Teqe) was a major centre of the sect, and many of its Babas were significant figures in the wider Bektashi movement. The remains of seven domed turbes, or tombs, can be seen on the hill. The principal turbe contains the relics of three important Dervishes: Babas Ibrahim, Suleiman and Seifulla. The main living complex is in serious disrepair, and the current incumbent, Baba Skender, lives in a new house nearby.

Numbers in this section refer to the map inside the front cover

Left Gjirokastra mosque destroyed by the communists (A. Q. SH. i R. SH. Fototeka) *Right* Meçites Mosque, or Seven Fountains mosque, destroyed in 1967 (A. Q. SH. i R. SH. Fototeka) *Below* Hill of Tuff Teqe (A. Q. SH. i R. SH. Fototeka)

Old Quarters tour: Dunavat and Manalat

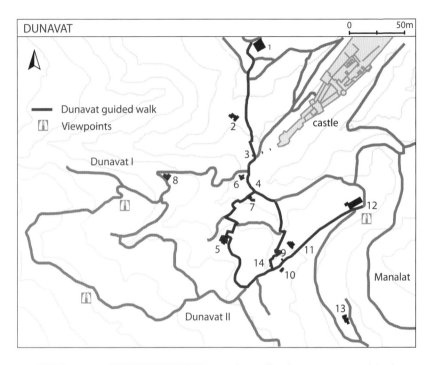

This walk takes you to two of the less-visited quarters of Gjirokastra, Dunavat and Manalat. These residential districts are full of the city's characteristic tower houses and provide wonderful views of the city and its surroundings. Topography makes them difficult to see from the rest of Gjirokastra although they constitute a large proportion of the historic city. The walk follows the many secondary pathways and alleys for a relatively traffic-free tour. Allow about 50 minutes to complete the route.

Numbers correspond to the Dunavat map in this chapter.

Left Remains of the aqueduct piers at the base of the castle mount

View of Dunavat from the castle

Start in front of the Bazaar mosque (1), take the narrow cobbled road that leads up to the right of the mosque and follow this to the junction at the top. Here roads lead left to the Odeon and castle, and right up to the Palorto quarter and the Zekate House, while a much narrower cobbled path leads straight ahead and upwards. Take this path, it is generally well paved although steep in places. Up to the right, one can see glimpses of the Kabilate House (2).

At the top of the path some steps lead up the final distance to the concrete road at the top, cross over the road and stop by the stone wall on the far side. The castle rises steeply above. Beside you in the wall, there is a block of masonry that is distinctly different from those nearby. This is the base of one of the piers of Ali Pasha's aqueduct, other (reconstructed) pier bases can be seen up on the left on the lower slopes of the castle hill (3).

A little further on is a junction with roads leading left and right. High up in front a single restored house stands out, this is the Topulli House (5), your immediate destination. The road to the right leads up through the Dunavat quarter, but it is steep and windy. In preference, proceed along the left-hand road and walk to the foot of the Rruga Ago Topulli (4), which is a stepped path that leads up to the right of the road to the Topulli House.

Dunavat tower houses

On the right-hand side of the junction is a communist-era partisan memorial. A little further, on the right, there is the small but well preserved Kavate House, with its gated and walled yard (6). Start climbing the Rruga Ago Topulli and on the left you will pass the impressive Sinani House (7). Built in 1872, it was one of the last houses of its kind. The layout comprises a series of rooms arranged around a single divan, rather than the traditional multipurpose rooms. This arrangement represents the gradual adoption of western ideas of housing and the concomitant changes in Albanian social structure (see page 41).

Above Topulli House
Below Kikino House detail

At the first junction take the paved path that leads to the left, and then shortly afterwards the right-hand path up the well-built steps. Looking to the right at this point across the small valley gives a fine view of the houses, amongst which is the Beqiri House, as yet unrestored and still used as a private residence **(8)**. It stands proud on the upper right-hand side with a jettied roof. At the top of these steps is the restored Topulli House set among pine and spruce trees. The house was rebuilt under the communists to act as the historical museum of Albanian independence. Originally it was the family home of the Topulli clan whose most famous member, Çerçiz Topulli, led a band of freedom fighters during the early years of the 20th century (see page 17). The house has now been returned to its owners and is again a private residence.

Follow the concrete road to the left until you meet the principal asphalted road, turn left and head down into the second part of the Dunavat quarter (turn right for a lane with views of the castle and that leads back down through Dunavat to the top of the path by the aqueduct pier). On the left, the wall of the new Helveti dervish teqe soon comes into view **(9)**. The Helveti is a Sufi sect originally from Turkey which spread its message not only through teaching but also through music and dance. The sect has recently taken over the maintenance of the Dunavat mosque, which stands opposite the teqe, and it is hoped it will fully restore the mosque **(10)**.

Above Dunavat quarter
Below Dunavat mosque pre-1967

Kikino House

The mosque lost its minaret in the anti-religious campaigns of 1967, the main building survived and was used as a store room. An inscription over the doorway records its construction. The building is quite small and simple with a tiled cupola rising from square outer walls; the interior retains traces of decorative spandrels around the base of the dome and a carved mihrab in the eastern wall. A pathway to the right of the mosque allows a good view of the structure from the rear.

Proceeding down the road towards the yellow-painted Naim Frasheri school you will pass a series of bunkers on the right with attached concrete vaults that acted as accommodation and stores for the troops who would have been stationed here (11).

From the top of the bunkers there is a good view down into Manalat and beyond to the now abandoned communist Industrial Zone, and across the valley to Antigoneia on the far side. You could walk to the school and take the road down into the quarter (12). Manalat is isolated from the rest of the city by the intervening hill and in the 19th century it housed a self-contained community that took less interest in the day to day affairs of Gjirokastra than communities from the more central quarters.

There are a number of tower houses in Manalat, the most impressive of which is the Kikino House **(13)**. Built in 1825 with three floors, including storage rooms, winter and summer quarters, it was owned by a wealthy Christian family. At the time it was built this would have been the outer edge of the city and this imposing structure would have dominated the neighbourhood as the Manalat quarter grew up around it.

Retrace your steps back up the road past the Helveti teqe and turn right down the path beyond. This leads down past an ancient octagonal turbe (a Dervish's tomb), part of the teqe, and through an arched opening **(14)**. Follow the path down the hill and some very fine views of the castle open up in front. The path goes straight down to the road (ignore the left-hand pathway which returns up to the Topulli House). Turn left, and it is easy to navigate back down to the starting point at the mosque in the Bazaar.

Left View of the castle from Dunavat
Below Tower house

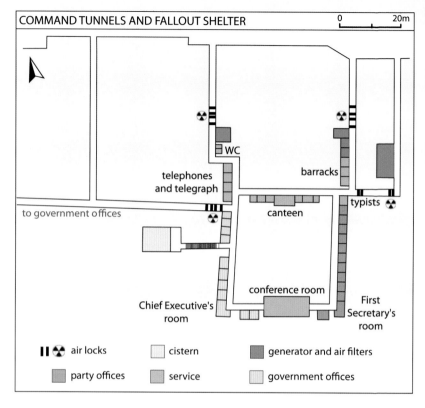

COMMAND TUNNELS AND FALLOUT SHELTER

0   20m

WC

telephones
and telegraph

barracks

to government offices

typists

canteen

conference room

Chief Executive's
room

First
Secretary's
room

air locks   cistern   generator and air filters

party offices   service   government offices

Given its strategic position in communist Albania, Gjirokastra was equipped with a full range of modern defences and wartime shelters for both the army and civilians. Ideally, every citizen was supposed to be able to reach a shelter within three minutes of an alarm sounding, and regular exercises were held across the country. A walk around the town will reveal many passageways leading up into the hillsides, as well as numerous bunkers dotted in strategic positions. Please be very careful if entering any of these, as they have long been abandoned and can be hazardous and unpleasant.

The communist command tunnels are better preserved than most of the other defensive structures, and a section of the network is expected to be opened soon to the public as a Cold War museum. Built during the 1970s and 80s, this underground system was tunnelled under the castle hill with entrances from behind the Party offices (now the Town Hall) and the regional government building. As a centre of regional government, Gjirokastra needed to maintain a balance between the Party and various government bodies. The tunnel system reflected this and consisted of two identical sections: one for Party functionaries and officers, the other for their corresponding government colleagues. The offices of the First Secretary and the Chief Executive, for example, are exactly the same shape and size and are all connected at shared conference room, canteen and toilets.

The entire network was also equipped with separate cisterns, generators and air filtration systems. Massive blast doors and airlocks sealed the various entrances and internal air pressure would be kept slightly higher to keep out potentially radioactive particles. As an extra precaution, the generator and electrical system could be isolated to protect against electromagnetic pulses, which would be generated by a possible nuclear explosion.

The individual rooms, offices and barracks were lined with concrete and simply furnished with basic lighting. Furniture was utilitarian, and consisted of metal bunks, a table, chairs and wooden stools.

Although never pressed into active service, the tunnels were used regularly for exercises and drills, and it is still possible to find ex-party or local government officials who know what it was like to be shut behind the thick blast-proof doors.

Below Pedestrian passageway leading under the castle *Right* Inside the communist command tunnels

Excursions in the Gjirokastra region

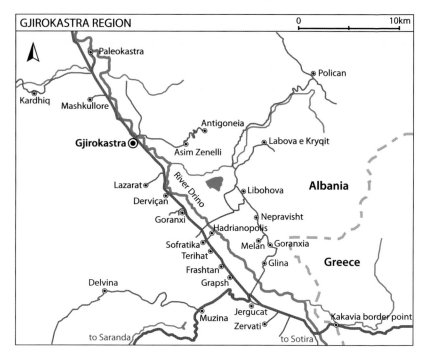

GJIROKASTRA REGION
0   10km

Paleokastra
Polican
Kardhiq   Mashkullore
Antigoneia
Gjirokastra ⊙   Labova e Kryqit
Asim Zenelli
Lazarat   River Drino   Libohova   **Albania**
Derviçan
Goranxi   Nepravisht
Hadrianopolis
Sofratika   Melan Goranxia
Terihat
Frashtan   Glina   **Greece**
Delvina   Grapsh
Jergucat
Muzina   Kakavia border point
Zervati
to Saranda   to Sotira

Carpet weaver, Antigoneia

Visiting the many historical sites in the Drino Valley is also an opportunity to enjoy the beautiful countryside. Views of the mountains and the lush valley are features of every excursion, while the destinations tell the story of this area, from prehistory to modern times. The region is largely unspoilt with little modern development away from the main highway. While this gives a feel for a traditional Albanian way of life, the unmade roads can be perilous to cars.

If you want to make touring the region a feature of your visit to Gjirokastra, it is advisable to use a four-wheel drive vehicle, or hire a taxi (see page 84). Each of the excursions are described as separate trips, however some of them can be combined and several can be completed in one day. For directions, please refer to the map entitled 'Gjirokastra Region' in this chapter.

From Gjirokastra to Antigoneia
Journey time: 45 mins
A four-wheel drive vehicle is advisable.

Take the eastern road from the roundabout in lower Gjirokastra (**18** Shtatori quarter); take the first turn to the right after the bridge and continue to the village of Asim Zeneli, the largest village in the Commune of Antigone. This well-organised village was founded after the Second World War by a migrant community from the mountainous area of Kurvelesh. Traditionally a sheep-farming area, the first stock-farming cooperative in Albania was established here soon after the beginning of communist rule. Kurvelesh provided the Partisan movement with numerous soldiers and there is a statue to commemorate the hero-shepherd in the square at Asim Zeneli. The office of the National Archaeological Park of Antigoneia is located at the centre of the village, next to the Commune offices, in which guides and information can be found. From here it is possible to hike up to Antigoneia. To drive, (see page 78) pass through the village and follow the road ahead. At the next village of Krina, bear right through the square, past the ancient plane tree, and continue along the unpaved and sometimes rough track. Eventually the road approaches the village of Saraqinishta and there is a track signposted to the right leading to the hill of Jerme and the ancient city Antigoneia.

Antigoneia

In Saraqinishta, there are two 17th-century churches that are well worth visiting. Shën Koll (Saint Nicholas) was constructed between 1620 and 1630. Notice the dedication to the painter-decorators above the door. The walls are the work of the 17th-century painter Michael of Linotopi, while the icons of the iconsatasis (now missing) included panels by the well-known 17th-century icon painter Nikolla, son of Onufri. Some spolia from the ruins of Antigoneia are incorporated in the walls, and several columns stand in the churchyard. The interior is accessed by a long, covered narthex with a wonderful wooden arcade and roof.

The main church is subdivided by columns that support the dome in the form of a Greek cross. The second 17th-century church, Shën Merisë (Saint Mary), was decorated in 1613 by Alebiozius Phokas. The church is a rectangular basilica of typical southern Albanian form with a long open porch on its southern side.

The custodian will be happy to open up for you. His house, with a colossal ancient tree in the middle of its courtyard, is easy to spot.

Above Remains of the city walls, Antigoneia

Antigoneia, the dream of King Pyrrhus

Antigoneia was founded by King Pyrrhus of Epirus (319-272 BC), from whom we gain the expression 'a Pyrrhic victory', (a victory achieved at such cost that its worth is questionable) after his disastrous invasion of Italy. The city was named after his wife, Antigone, who was the step-daughter of King Ptolemy of Egypt, one of Alexander the Great's generals. Pyrrhus wanted to consolidate his kingdom against the tribal neighbours to the north, and sponsored a new city to bring together the scattered settlements of the valley.

A cousin of Alexander the Great, Pyrrhus led a colourful life as a mercenary, general and later King of Epirus, which he raised briefly to the status of a great power. Antigoneia flourished from the 4th to 2nd centuries BC and Epirus had become allied with the Kingdom of Macedonia in their wars against the rising power of the Roman Republic. Following the final defeat of King Philip V of Macedonia in 168 BC, the Roman Consul Aemilius Paullus ordered the destruction of all of the cities of Epirus as punishment. Antigoneia was one of these cities, deliberately razed and its inhabitants sold into slavery.

It is possible to see the excavated remains of a number of sections of Antigoneia. The Albanian archaeologist Dhimosten Budina first identified the ruins of the ancient city, known only from historical sources, after discovering a series of bronze tokens with the Greek word 'Antigoneiaon' stamped on them. These may have been used for balloting in the city assembly.

ANTIGONEIA

0   250m

entrance track

Most impressive are the walls that run along the western side of the city and around the acropolis at its northern end. The eastern side, protected by the almost sheer drop into the valley on this side of the town, appears to have been left without defensive structures. The walls were built of limestone blocks quarried from the nearby hillside. There are a number of noticeable gates, the most visible being at the southwestern side of the city.

Following the path from the site gate the visitor first encounters the acropolis hill, with its light oak woods **(1)**. The track circles around and heads on through the lines of defensive walls into the city. Several houses have been excavated and in the city centre an entire section of the street grid is exposed **(2)**. The regular grid of the city streets follows the scheme for city planning first laid down by Hippodamus of Miletus in the 5th century BC. The first house on the left of the track is the so-called 'peristyle house,' named for its central colonnaded courtyard **(4)**. The house was originally two storeys high, built largely of mud-brick and timber on stone foundations with an annexed storage yard. Beyond and to the west is the 'carpenter's house', named after the tools found here. The regular grid pattern of urban organisation is typically Hellenistic. Excavations in these houses and elsewhere produced clear evidence of the city's destruction - a thick layer of burning found within the buildings dated by pottery and coins, the fiery end of Antigoneia's short life.

The main track leads on, past an intersection and the ruins of a small medieval church, to the agora **(3)**. This open space would have been the focal point of city life and political organisation. Excavations found the remains of a bronze equestrian statue, possibly of Pyrrhus himself, that would have stood here. A series of stone buildings and covered colonnades stand on the massive artificial terrace specially constructed on the edge of the city overlooking the valley, over which there are fine views.

A walk to the southern end of the city passes other buildings, an impressive section of the city walls and a gateway. It is easy to see how both the gate and walls have been slighted, their upper levels pushed over down the slope. This was the work of Aemillius Paullus' army after 168BC. At the very end of the city, overlooking a spectacular drop, is a small early Christian church of triconch form **(5)**. This chapel is one of a few buildings that were constructed on this site after the burning of the city.

Libohova Castle

Libohova

Its position may have been chosen for its remoteness and it is likely to have been built as a small pilgrimage centre. A rough, interesting mosaic covers the floor of the triconch, featuring at its core the figure of Abraxas, the cock-headed fighter against evil, depicted in battle with a snake representing the powers of darkness. Other panels depict fish, a typical reference to Christianity and Christ. An encircling band of ivy leaves forms the border while a series of Greek inscriptions name the donors who have paid for the church and floor and presumably the maintenance of the priest: "The slave of God, Agathokles, made this in fulfillment of a vow". The finds from Antigoneia are in Tirana at the National History Museum and the National Archaeological Museum.

From Gjirokastra to Libohova
Journey time: 30 mins

Libohova is one of the most interesting and attractive villages of the region. Take the main road south from Gjirokastra towards Kakavia, after about 15 kms take the sign-posted road to the east across the valley that winds up into the town.

Libohova is nestled at the foot of Mount Bureto. The archaeological finds indicate it was the site of a very ancient settlement, which reached its height of prosperity after the 17th century. It is the traditional home of the Libohova family, one of the great families of landed 'Beys' who formed the Ottoman aristocracy. The entire town is spread out like a mini Gjirokastra on the mountainside.

Shanisha, like her brother, was by all accounts a formidable personality. Along with her mother she was once held captive by the people of Kardhiq resulting in a vow of vengeance from Ali that was carried out in a terrible fashion, it included stuffing the cushions in Shanisha's serai with the hair of the Kardhiqiote women. Whatever the truth of this grisly story, the castle dominated the village and ensured that the control of this side of the Drino Valley remained firmly in Ali's hands.

A number of traditional buildings survive among the paved inner lanes, which connect the upper and the lower quarters and ensure smooth driving all the way up to the top of the town. Two extraordinary towers are still standing and are the last remains of a unique local architectural tradition.

Libohova Castle is the town's main attraction. This is a substantial fortress with four polygonal corner towers with vaulted interiors and a curtain wall surrounding a wide courtyard. The only gate lies on the northern side and is accessed along a lane against a private house. The lane is normally used as a chicken coop and may be blocked by a wire gate - however, the owners are happy for visitors to enter. The castle was the dowry that Ali Pasha presented to his sister, Shanisha, who married one of the most important members of the Libohova family. Her grave is in the southern part of the village. The large raised platform in the centre of the castle is most likely the site of her serai (palace court).

The high street has a number of fine plane and mulberry trees. The largest, an enormous 300 year-old plane tree, casts a very large and cool patch of shade, being 32 m high, with a trunk 6.9 m in circumference, and a crown as great as 80 m across. Nearby is a bubbling mountain spring, and it is hard to resist having a drink at the adjacent bar and enjoying this very pleasant mountain village.

At the centre of the main street lies the house of Myfit Bey Libohova (1876–1927), a renowned politician. In the first government of independent Albania, formed in 1912, he became the Minister of Internal and Foreign Affairs. His nephews are currently reconstructing his large house to its original glory.

You could continue this excursion with a trip to Labova e Kryqit, described below. Leave Libohova as if to return to Gjirokastra, but take the right turn to Suha, just a short distance from the town.

Above Labova e Kryquit

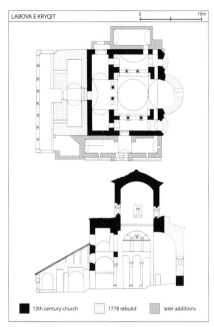

LABOVA E KRYQIT

0   10m

13th century church   1778 rebuild   later additions

To Labova e Kryqit
Journey time: 40 mins

The Church of Labova e Kryqit is one of the most interesting monuments in Albania. Leave Gjirokastra and follow the route to Libohova (see page 67). Before reaching Libohova take a left-hand fork on an asphalt road towards Suha. The asphalt surface will give out after a few kilometres, but the unpaved road is quite passable. At the next junction keep to the right and the road will start to wind uphill. Keep on this road, ignore the various divisions and forks as they all link up again. As you approach the village of Labova e Kryqit the asphalt surface recommences. Follow the road into the centre where the church is situated.

Below Mountain view

The Church of Labova e Kryqit is one of the oldest in Albania, and allegedly contained a wooden fragment of the original cross. The building is typically Byzantine with a high central cupola, and a nave and aisles arranged in cruciform plan. A narthex, added later, provides the principal entrance. There are up to nine distinct levels of fresco painting on the interior walls. The church is essentially 13th-century, from the time of the Despots of Epirus, although an original foundation may go back to AD 527-565 and the reign of Emperor Justinian. The keys are held by the custodian who lives across the street.

On the mountain slopes above the village it is possible to pick out with binoculars the ruins of a substantial pre-Roman fortification. A difficult scramble taking about 30 minutes over rocky slopes will take you up to the walls, which are comprised of polygonal and rectangular hewn blocks with a circular tower at the northwest corner.

Above Fresco of Christ, Labova e Kryqit

To the Teqe of Melan
Journey time: 50 mins

To get to Melan take the road to Glina east from the National Road approximately 20 km south of Gjirokastra. The road runs up to the bottling plant of the famous Glina mineral water, which can be seen from across the valley. Take the road behind the plant that has a concrete paved surface for a few kilometres and leads through the villages perched on the side of the mountain. Continue straight on and resist all temptation to take tracks or roads to the side even though the middle way narrows considerably when it reaches the village of Grapsh, 4 km from Glina. From here the road descends in curves to the Teqe of Melan, which is entered alongside a small aqueduct that originally brought water to the shrine. The grove of tall ancient Cyprus trees is clearly visible from the track and also from the valley below.

The site has a long history. A massive wall of polygonal and rectangular blocks encircles the end of the promontory, suggesting an Epirot or Illyrian fortification. This idea is supported by finds of particular ceramics from the 4th century BC. The wall was reconstructed in the 5th or 6th centuries AD when many of these ancient hilltop sites were refortified as the Roman Empire declined. It is one of the possible locations of the city of Justinianopolis. Melan may also have been a fortified site in the middle ages as a small single-nave church exists in the undergrowth on the southern side of the fortified enclosure. A cobbled road takes visitors up to the Teqe of Melan, past a fine Ottoman-period fountain that was the original destination of the aqueduct. At present, the teqe serves as a religious centre for the Bektashi Shia Muslims and there is a Baba in permanent residence.

Above Teqe of Melan

The present teqe buildings were erected in 1800 by Baba Ali from Gjirokastra, whose tomb is contained in the turbe in front of the main structure. Constructed in typically southern Albanian-style with locally quarried well-cut stone blocks, it consists of a circular prayer hall with annexed rooms and galleries.

The buildings we see today are a reconstruction of an earlier Bektashi teqe, which was led by Baba Hasan. At an even earlier phase, a Christian complex, which consisted of a monastery, existed. It should be noted that this site would not have been as remote as it is today; it lies on the original route through the Drino Valley that kept to higher ground, the same one that the English Baron Cam Hobhouse passed in 1809 with his friend Lord Byron during their journey to visit Ali Pasha at Tepelena.

Subsequently Ali Pasha erected a series of bridges and causeways across the river and flood plains of the valley floor after 1811, forming a new and easier road.

From Gjirokastra to Dropull -
exploring the villages
Journey time: a whole day to see them all

Many of the villages south of Gjirokastra on the west side of the National Road, an area known as Dropull, are populated by a Greek minority. The first village you pass is Lazarat, which is inhabited by ethnic Albanians. The well-known Bektashi Teqe of Baba Zenel, thought to have been built in the 18th century, lies in the upper quarter of this village

Driving south, on your right you will see the Greek minority villages of Derviçan, Goranxi, and Sofratika, coming into view one after the other. Derviçan is the largest of the three, and is situated 1 km west from the National Road. The main village church is a recently restored 18th-century building that was used as a warehouse during the communist regime. The Church of Shën Ana (Saint Anna) is located on a plateau on higher ground, among a number of other ruined buildings. This church is very old, possibly dating from the 15th century when nearly 700 households lived here. The surrounding ruins suggest that the village once extended across the plateau. The Church of Burimi Jetëdhënës (Life-giving Spring), not far from Shën Anna, was built in the same period. Another important piece of the local architectural heritage is the 17th-century house of Zaharo Sterjo built entirely of stone laid without mortar. It is related in style to the fortified dwellings found in Gjirokastra.

Above Fountain, Teqe of Melan
Left Teqe of Melan

The village of Goranxi is 2 km further south. The principal church, Shën Mëria (Saint Mary), dates to 1600, although a 1995 fire destroyed several parts of the building. Also worth visiting is Goranxi gorge, which is just to the north of the village and dramatically cuts into the mountainside. A small late Byzantine church with frescoes lies on a rise near the mouth of the gorge. Further along, on the northern side, is one of the most remarkable prehistoric archaeological sites of the region, a flint quarry composed of several rock shelters carved into the side of the gorge during the Upper Paleolithic and Mesolithic periods (c. 25000-7000 BC). The quarries themselves are still visible in the flint-bearing strata on the northern gorge wall. Among the remains of this ancient industry are a number of stone-built dwellings dating from the Hellenistic and Roman periods.

Further south, Sofratika contains characteristic architecture partially built over the necropolis of the Roman city of Hadrianopolis. The city was constructed by Emperor Hadrian in the 2nd century AD with the likely intention to bring together the scattered communities of the valley who had been without a focal point since the destruction of Antigoneia some 400 years previously. Turn right off the National Road and immediately left along a road running parallel to the highway. A small tunnel leads east under the National Road and out into the flood plain of the Drinos. The track is passable, though the tunnel can be a tight fit for large vehicles. If you prefer to park, the site is a 10 minute walk from there. Follow the track to a series of isolated plane trees, and the principal ruins are on your right. The most impressive feature is a small well-preserved Roman theatre, with a cavea, orchestra and scena frons.

Above Hadrianopolis
Below Rock shelter at Goranxi

Nearby are some excavated houses and other buildings. The city was never large and appears to have been deliberately designed only to provide city centre services, while the population remained living in the older villages and townships of the surrounding hills and valleys. Hadrianopolis was probably abandoned after the 6th century AD.

Continuing southwards, the next village of Jergucat is located at the junction with the road to Saranda. The tall church of Shën Kozma (Saint Cosmas) appears a little before a bend in the road. By the eastern side of the main highway road before the Saranda turn-off are the remains of a large Macedonian-style monumental tomb from the 3rd century BC, which was found during the road's construction. The main tomb chamber survives as does the partly-restored access stairway.

There are a number of other villages worth visiting while on the way to the Kakavia border. Several kilometres south of Jergucat is the village of Zervat, the site of a 10th-century church devoted to Saint Mary. Further on, in the village of Dhuvjan, there is a 16th-century monastery. At Panaja, there is 10th-century church encircled by a high wall of cypresses, which was the ancient centre of the Bishop of Drinopull. It is one of the oldest and most interesting churches in the Lower Peshkëpi area, close to the border with Greece. Along a side road from the main highway just before Kakavia lies the village of Sotira, a Greek minority settlement and almost as far south as one can go in modern Albania. The mountains of the frontier are visible through the ancient oak and plane woods. The village is delightful with a 13th-century monastery at the centre. Near the fresh spring is another mighty plane tree, around 300 years old.

Left Bell tower at St. Paul's church, Terihat
Above Grapsh church

PALEOKASTRA

0   50m

churches

River Drino

to
Gjirokastra

buildings

From Gjirokastra to Paleokastra and Kardhiq

Journey time: 30 mins to Paleokastra, 1hr to Kardhiq

Take the National Road north from Gjirokastra past Viroi Lake and continue towards Tepelena. A 20 minute drive will bring you to a crossroads on the main highway. The right-hand turn goes to Paleokastra, the left to the Kardhiq valley.

Paleokastra

Follow the road to the right and continue straight on, do not turn into the village of Paleokastra, but carry on along the unpaved track. About 10 minutes after leaving the National Road, the fortress of Paleokastra comes into view. Its name means 'old castle'

and this ancient fortress dates to the Roman period. It is one of the few Roman military installations to be seen in this area of the Balkans. It is thought to have been built in the 4th century AD, at the time of Emperor Constantine the Great (272-337 AD), to house a cavalry company. The collapsed walls are easily traceable; the rectangular shape of a typical Roman fortress can be seen with angular corner towers and a single gate to the west. Excavations have shown that it remained in use well into the 6th century AD, and later additions include two small churches built within the walls. The fort was undoubtedly placed here to guard both the river as well as the entrance to the Kardhiq valley, through which ran the main Roman road to Saranda and the coast.

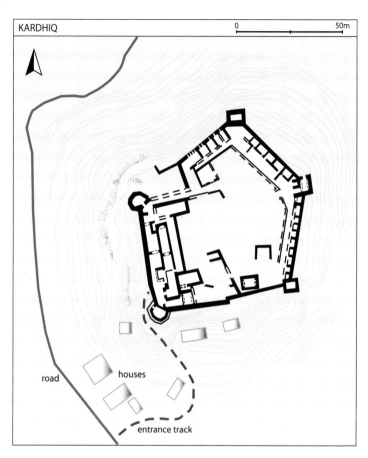

KARDHIQ   0   50m

road   houses

entrance track

Kardhiq

Taking the left-hand turn off the National Road leads up and over a spur of the hill into the Kardhiq valley. The road soon loses its asphalt and becomes a bumpy dirt track. Originally this valley was the main routeway to the coast with roads and tracks leading over the mountains to the south, via the pass of Scafica, to the Saranda region, or north to Borsh. Today it is something of a backwater, although there are plans to route a new highway through here.

A number of villages remain in the valley but the principal reason for a visit is to see the evocative ruins of Kardhiq. These are positioned on a hill in the centre of the valley on the banks of the river Belice. The road winds up the northern face of the hill. Kardhiq was a large open town with a fortress, similar to Gjirokastra, but smaller. It was self-governing, wealthy and controlled the trade routes over the mountains. These reasons alone might have been sufficient to arouse the ire

of Ali Pasha who desired control of its territory and its commerce, but in addition, the Kardhiqiotes had once captured and assaulted his mother and sister. Eventually with the growing power of the Pasha, Ali gained control of the town. His revenge was terrible. He reputedly had 700 descendents of those who had insulted his family massacred in an inn by the Gjirokastra road, and their wives and children sold into slavery.

While the fortress of Kardhiq was extensively rebuilt (most of the surviving circuit and towers are the work of Ali Pasha's engineers), the town declined following his atrocity with the bulk of its population moving to Gjirokastra. The extensive jumble of ruins, the remains of the town, can be seen on the slope opposite the fortress. Walls of houses and the stumps of minarets are all visible.

Hiking in the Gjirokastra region
The countryside surrounding Gjirokastra is beautiful and there is the potential for some very enjoyable hiking in the valley. Walking as a leisure pursuit, however, is not a popular Albanian pastime, and there are no developed tourist trails in the area. Fortunately, there are a number of walkable paths that can be used to visit some of the destinations discussed in this chapter.

Visitors adventurous enough to seek out these walks should refer to Trekking Through Southern Albania (Hayden, 2005), available from the Tourist Information Centre in Gjirokastra.

Above Kardhiq castle
Below Walking to Antigoneia from Gjirokastra

One of the more accessible routes is from Gjirokastra to Antigoneia. It takes about two hours (four hour round trip) making a decent day outing when coupled with a picnic among the ancient ruins. On the ridge above the western side of the valley, there is a track cut during the communist era intended for military vehicles. It was never used for this purpose, but there are paths up to it from Goranxi, Lazarat and Gjirokastra, as well as paths down into the next valley to Leferohori village and the town of Delvina. This communist track begins at the mouth of the Kardhiq valley and runs south to meet the Jergucat to Saranda road near Kardhikaqi. There are other paths leading south from further up the Kardhiq valley, as well as possibilities for walking on the Paleokastra side of the National Road.

Sensible precautions must be taken when venturing into the Albanian mountains, especially in a country with poor infrastructure and emergency services. Proper walking boots are essential, along with a basic first aid kit, plenty to drink and eat as well as large-scale maps of the area. It is also advisable to let someone know your route and expected time of return. With careful planning, the walks can be immensely rewarding with stunning views, a rich array of flowers, birds and animals, remote villages, and, of course, a great sense of achievement at the end of an enjoyable day.

Top left Communist bunker
Bottom left Bridge over the River Drinos
Top right Kelcyre gorge, near Tepelena
Above River Drinos

Iso-polyphonic singing

Iso-polyphonic singing is the traditional folk music of Albania. There are different styles practiced in the north and south of the country but all consist of a blend of voices including a melody and a counter melody, sung as solos, and a choral drone. In the south the Tosks sing a continuous choral drone on the syllable 'e', staggering their breathing so as not to break the note. Also from the south, the Labs perform a more rhythmic drone that follows the text of the song. Traditionally, iso-polyphony is a male pursuit but occasionally a woman may join in, often singing a melody.

Albanians are proud of their tradition and it remains an integral part of their social lives. Especially in the south it is performed, often impromptu, at weddings, funerals, harvest feasts, religious celebrations and other gatherings, and you may hear a band of shepherds singing in the hills or a group of friends singing in a restaurant after a meal. Organised groups, dressed in regional costume, will sing at more formal events, and singers from across the country and the Albanian diaspora, gather every four years to celebrate their art at the National Folk Festival held in the castle at Gjirokastra. Employed by Enver Hoxha as part of his policy to promote a feeling of national solidarity, iso-polyphony was hailed during his premiership as an element of true Albanian people's culture.

Consequently, it has become engrained in the Albanian sense of national identity, which has done much to keep the tradition vibrant and creative. Proclaimed as an 'intangible cultural heritage' by UNESCO in 2005, Albanian iso-polyphony is now gaining recognition and popularity outside of Albania.

The origins of Albanian iso-polyphony are unclear but evidence suggests it has a long history. One legend tells that, when a ship arrived at Lake Butrint bringing news of the death of Pan, the people spontaneously moaned in unison, singing a requiem to the great god. There are numerous literary and artistic depictions of Albanian singers by travellers to the region indicating both the prevalence of the tradition and the impact it had on visitors. An early reference is in Evliya Çelebi's Book of Travels published in 1670. Çelebi was a traveller who journeyed for over 40 years through the Ottoman territories and beyond. He records in his notes on Gjirokastra that, "The people of Gjirokastra mourn their dead relatives for forty of fifty, indeed up to eighty years… For this reason I dubbed Gjirokastra the 'city of wailing'. It is a great wonder how the professional mourners manage to weep and wail with such feeling."

The more sombre iso-polyphonic songs can indeed be very sorrowful and quite moving even without understanding the lyrics. The atmosphere created by the choral background and the often enchanting dialogue of two solo melodies creates a captivating and enveloping sound. The old songs continue to be passed down the generations, while modern compositions concerning current issues keep the tradition vibrant. The verse from the lament below expresses the sorrow of a family separated when the sons emigrated.

I have a song to sing,
I sing of a broken heart,
Of a wasting illness,
A legacy of our past,
Cry, cry, oh my heart!
Mourn, mourn old mother of mine,
For the journey your sons have taken,
To leave our land and never
again return.
Our mothers cry with my words:
Our sons travel far across the world,
Their legs bear them onwards,
But they return only upon the wings
of death.

Cry oh Broken Heart
The Ionian Song
The Delvina Group 1994-95

Visiting Gjirokastra

People and Lifestyle

Albanians in general, and the people of Gjirokastra in particular, are delighted to have foreign visitors. This welcoming and protective attitude toward foreigners comes from a traditional custom of hospitality that is still particularly prevalent among older Albanians. Consequently, Gjirokastra has yet to acquire the attributes of the typical tourist trap town and, for the most part, people will not take advantage of tourists with high prices and poor value.

The town and the region have a harmonious mix of religions, despite many decades of communist state - enforced atheism. Muslims, Orthodox Christians, Catholics and Bektashi live side by side and a number of important and historic religious sites, such as the Church of Labova e Kryqit and the Bektashi Teqe of Melan can be found close to Gjirokastra (see page 62).

While the new town of Gjirokastra bustles with commerce, the hinterland is famed for its agriculture. The region supports many orchards, vineyards and tobacco plantations while the rich mountain pastures produce excellent livestock. Gjirokastra cheese, meat and honey are among the best in Albania.

Gjirokastra is the centre of Gjirokastra District, which includes the town of Libohova and communes of Antigone, Lower Dropull, Upper Dropull, Lazarat, Lunxheria, Odrie, Picar, Pogon, Qender Libohova, and Zagori. According to the 2001 Census, the official population is 35,000, living in an area of just over 4 km square, consisting of majority Albanians and minority Greeks, as well as a small community of Vlachs (a traditionally nomadic people who speak a Latin language similar to Romanian)

based mainly in the Commune of Odrie, in Andon Poçi village. Many people from the surrounding areas have emigrated to Greece to look for work and depopulated villages are common.

Visas

Citizens of the following nations are not required to obtain a visa in advance: Australia, Canada, Croatia, the European Union, Japan, New Zealand, Norway, San Marino, South Korea, Switzerland, Turkey and the United States of America. Visitors will be charged a €10 entry tax on arrival in Albania, although Czech and Polish citizens are exempt. The Albanian Foreign Ministry website (www.mfa.gov.al) has the latest travel information in both English and Albanian.

Left Gjirokastra new town *Bottom left* Folk dancing at a festival *Bottom right* Local traditional costumes

Getting There and Leaving

Gjirokastra is in the south of Albania, situated on the east face of the steep Mali i Gjerë (Wide Mountains) mountain range. It lies 232 km from Tirana, the capital and the location of the Mother Theresa Airport, the only international air terminal; 31 km from the Greek border crossing at Kakavia; and 56 km from Saranda, the seaport that connects the country, via a regular ferry service, to Corfu.

Gjirokastra sits just off the main north-south Albanian highway, Rruga Nacionale (National Road), which continues all the way to the Greek border. The highway from Tirana takes the following route - Tirana-Durrës-Kavaja-Rrogozhina-Lushnje-Fier-Ballsh-Mallakastra-Tepelena-Gjirokastra. By private car, this trip will take about 5 hours due to the poor condition of the roads. By bus, it will take 6 to 7 hours depending on how many stops the bus makes along the way. The ticket will cost Lek 1000.

Gjirokastra has regular bus services to Greek cities including Thessalonica, Ioannina and Athens. It is also well served by regular buses to Tirana, Vlora, Korça, Tepelena and Saranda. All buses for destinations inside Albania depart from a place called Agjencia, which is a wide spot in the National Road about 50 metres north of the roundabout in the new town. Check with your hotel or the Tourist Information Centre regarding departure times for your destination.

Weather

While a stay in Gjirokastra is worthwhile at any time of year, the best time to visit is in the spring when the fruit trees are in blossom and snow caps the mountains. It can be very hot in late summer, with temperatures rising to 36C, although the higher altitude of the old town means that the city is cooled by mountain breezes, especially in the evening. There are often clear warm days in both the autumn and the winter, although heavy rainfall is common in the latter and temperatures can drop below freezing at night. Precipitation ranges from 75 to 570 mm per month with most rain falling in the winter.

Practical Information

Electricity: The Albanian supply is 220 volts, 50 hertz, with a standard European two-pin plug. The voltage, however, is often far lower than 220 volts and power cuts are common, especially in the winter when demand increases. Surge protectors are recommended for all sensitive equipment such as computers. As the majority of the power in Albania is sourced from hydro-electric plants, long periods of drought can also disrupt supply.

Emergencies: Dial 129 for police emergencies, 124 for medical emergencies, and 0842 63333 for fire emergencies.

Health: The most common health problems encountered by foreigners in Albania are upset stomachs. It is best to be a little cautious, drink only bottled water and stick to the busier restaurants where the food will not have been left standing. Treatment for most minor ailments can be bought over-the-counter at the numerous pharmacies in Gjirokastra.

The pharmacist will be able to advise you. For more serious complaints or accidents there is a hospital in the new town.

Money: Albania's currency is the Lek, although Euros are widely used. You will need local currency in Gjirokastra, as not all businesses are prepared to accept Euros. Very few businesses accept credit cards in Gjirokastra. The best exchange rates are obtained through ATMs/bankomat machines, and there are plenty of them in the Main Boulevard in the new town. There are also two in the old town: one at the Raifeissen Bank near the Neck, and one on Varosh Street next to the Post Office. If you ask for your money in Lek 5,000 increments, you will probably receive Lek 5,000 notes, which can be difficult to change in smaller shops. Try asking for Lek 4,000 or 9,000 from the ATM to get smaller denominations.

Top left and centre The Neck of the Bazaar
Right New town shopping street

Taxi rank

Rental Cars: The nearest car rental outlets are in Tirana. If you intend to tour the region you should consider hiring a four wheel drive vehicle as many of the minor roads are unsurfaced and problematic for ordinary cars (see page 62). If you want to be driven around, you can hire a taxi with an Albanian driver. You will have to negotiate the price, but expect to pay about Lek 2000 per hour.

Post Office: The Post Office is located on Rruga Varosh. It is generally open Monday to Friday from 0830 to 1330, and 1430 to 1600. The customer service window is straight ahead from the entrance. The Albanian postal service is fine for sending postcards, but if you have important documents you may want to use DHL, which has an office on the main boulevard in the new town.

Shopping: Souvenir shopping is still quite limited in Albania and the few outlets for local crafts are concentrated around the Neck of the Bazaar.

The Qendra e Artizanit (Artisan Centre) on Castle Street near the Tourist Information Centre sells handmade crafts and other souvenirs from all over Albania, including traditional Gjirokastra wood carvings, stone carvings, lace and embroidery. Opened in 2007, the enterprise operates on a fair-trade basis, with all profits being returned to the producers.

Taxi Rank: Situated in Çerçiz Topulli Square, this is the only taxi rank in the old town. All taxi travel within the town costs Lek 300, although watch out for a tourist surcharge. Negotiate the price before you take the ride.

Time: Albania is one hour ahead of GMT from October to March and two hours ahead from April to September.

Tourist Information Centre: The Tourist Information Centre is on the left side of Castle Street up from the Neck of the Bazaar. Staff will be happy to help you organise your trip to Gjirokastra.
Open daily: 0900 to 1700
Telephone: +355 842 67077
Website: www.gjirokastra.org
Email: tic@gjirokastra.org

Accommodation
There are many hotels and guest houses in Gjirokastra - the few that stand out are listed below. A more comprehensive list can be found on the GCDO website: www.gjirokastra.org.

Hotel Çajupi
Çerçiz Topulli Square, old town.
This large hotel is currently being refurbished to international standards.

Situated in the heart of the old town opposite the taxi rank, it is ideally placed for those exploring the historic city. The hotel will be fully reopened in 2009.

Hotel Kalemi
Lagjia Palorto, old town.
Hotel Kalemi is a Gjirokastra tower house restored and converted by the owner into a delightfully rustic bed and breakfast with a pretty courtyard garden. There are beautiful views of the city and castle from most of its 10 rooms.
Tel: +355 842 63724 and +355 68 223 4373; fax +355 842 67260; http://hotelkalemi.tripod.com; draguak@yahoo.com
€30 per night for a double room including breakfast; cash only, (Lek, Euros, Dollars).

Amenities: parking; laundry; air conditioning; central heating; television.

Hotel Bleta
Lagjia 18, Shtatori, new town.
A mid-range hotel with 15 rooms near the Camille Stefani restaurant just off the main boulevard. The hotel entrance is to the side of the hotel's bar and patio.
Tel: +355 842 64714 & +355 68 205 5819; www.hotelbleta.net; info@hotelbleta.net
Rooms from €20 per night including breakfast. Ensuite and family rooms, some with balconies are available; cash only, Lek, Euros.
Amenities: modem internet access; bar; parking; laundry; air conditioning; central heating; telephone; television; hairdryer; refrigerator.

Old bazaar and castle

New bazaar restaurant

Hotel Number One

Lagjia 18, Shtatori, new town.
A mid-range hotel with 10 rooms near
the main boulevard.
Tel +355 84 63163
Rooms from €20 per night, 10 units;
cash only, Lek, Euros.
Amenities: modem internet access;
bar; restaurant; parking; laundry; air
conditioning; central heating;
telephone; television.

Eating Out

Gjirokastra cuisine reflects the region's
history of invasion and occupation.
Flavours and styles brought by the
Turks have been incorporated into
what is now traditional Albanian home
cooking. There are also many
similarities with Greek cuisine, and
even the typical salad of tomatoes,
cucumber and feta cheese is known in
Albania as "Greek Salad." The Italian
influence is perhaps the least integrated,
but extremely popular with pasta dishes
and pizzas available at most restaurants.
Lamb tends to be the preferred meat,
and it is often served simply cooked
with side dishes of potatoes and salad
or cooked vegetables.

For traditional meals of the region, try
tavë kosi, a delicious ovenbaked dish
of lamb with yoghurt and rice,
Pashaqofte, a soup made with small
meat balls, or qifqi, rice balls fried
with herbs and spices. For a savoury
snack, try a byrek, a flaky pastry pasty
filled with feta cheese, meat or
spinach. Often sold from a kiosk, the
byrek is traditional Albanian fast food.
For those with a sweet tooth, sample
the Turkish style baklava pastries filled
with almond or pistachio paste and
soaked in syrup.

The Language - spelling and pronunciation

Most people from Gjirokastra speak the southern Tosk dialect of Albanian. Greek is understood and spoken by many, while young people are also likely to speak English and Italian.

Spelling of place names: The Albanian is an inflected language, which means the endings of names change according to their context. For example, the capital city is spelt 'Tiranë' when written in a map, but 'Tirana' in the sentence 'I am going to Tirana'. In some contexts, it can even be 'Tiranës'. Be prepared to encounter a variety of endings on your travels!

In this guide, the following conventions are used:
-a is used for names that end in ë or a, e.g. Tirana, Korça
-ra is used for names that end in ër or ra, eg. Gjirokastra, Dobra
-i after a final consonant is not used, e.g. Ksamil, Konispol, Piqeras

Craft fair

Pronunciation: The Albanian alphabet has 36 letters, containing all the Latin letters except W, as well as an additional 11 letters, most of which are double letters representing a single sound. The list below shows the variations between Albanian and English pronunciation:

a	–	as in father	o	–	as in open
c	–	as in tsar	q	–	as in mature
ç	–	as in chain	rr	–	as in rolled
dh	–	as in they	th	–	as in thick
e	–	as in pen	u	–	as in put
ë	–	as in around	x	–	as in adze
gj	–	as in judge	xh	–	as in fudge
i	–	as in police	y	–	as in French 'tu'
j	–	as in yellow	z	–	as in zero
ll	–	as in little	zh	–	as in pleasure
nj	–	as in union			

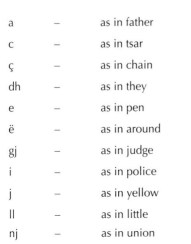

Walking on cobblestones

Castle road cobbles

Most of the cobblestone streets in Gjirokastra are paved with an attractive mix of pink, white and black stones. The pink and white cobbles are both limestone, the pink being formed by the natural leaching of iron oxides. The black stones are shale, and come from a quarry across the valley in the Lunxheria Mountains. When it rains (and it often does in the winter), the pink and white stones are very slippery - stick to the rougher black ones, which have much better traction. Also, present day heavy vehicle traffic and old cobblestones don't mix, the result being potholes and rough patches - watch your step!

While the cobblestones are the traditional form of paving, many of the outlying paths and streets were surfaced for the first time in the late 1970s when Enver Hoxha made his final visit to the city of his birth. This systematic paving of dirt alleys and paths was carried out as part of a "Peoples' initiative", by "volunteer" youth groups to beautify the leader's city.

Volunteer youth group mending a road, 1970s

Relaying a cobbled road in preparations for Hoxha's visit to Gjirokastra, 1970s

Black and white cobblestones

Index